FROM ANCIENT ROME TO ROCK 'N' ROLL

A REVIEW OF THE UK LEISURE SECURITY INDUSTRY

Mick Upton

ENTERTAINMENT TECHNOLOGY PRESS

Security Series

This book is dedicated to the Nigel Browne, a true professional.
His tragic death in a helicopter crash on August 26th, 1990
was a loss to the security industry.

FROM ANCIENT ROME TO ROCK 'N' ROLL

A REVIEW OF THE UK LEISURE SECURITY INDUSTRY

Mick Upton

Entertainment Technology Press

From Ancient Rome to Rock 'n' Roll
A Review of the UK Leisure Security Industry

© Mick Upton

First edition published December 2007
by Entertainment Technology Press Ltd
The Studio, High Green, Great Shelford, Cambridge CB22 5EG
Internet: www.etnow.com

ISBN 978 1 904031 50 5

A title within the
Entertainment Technology Press Security Series
Series editor: John Offord

CODE / FAR

CONTENTS

FOREWORD 9

INTRODUCTION 11

1 THE BEGINNING 13

2 FROM MUSIC HALL TO ROCK 'N' ROLL 23

3 LONDON TO LOS ANGELES 39

4 ARTISTES SECURITY SERVICES 55

5 CREATING AN INDUSTRY 75
   Rock Steady 76
   ShowSec International 78
   Goldrange Ltd 84
   Show & Event 88
   Olympus Security 92
   Special Events Security Ltd 96

6 LEARNING FROM THE PAST 101
   Donington Monsters of Rock 1988 102
      Previous History of the Event 103
      The Venue 104
      The Police 105
      Pre-Planning 105
      The Show 106
      Incident #1 107
      Incident #2 108
      Incident #3 110
      The Inquest 111
      The Aftermath 111
   Disaster at the Atrock Festival 111
      The Concert 113
      Event Marketing 114
      The Incident 115

Aftermath 117
Private Security 117

7   GUIDANCE AND LEGISLATION 121
Published Guidance 121
Guide to Safety at Sports Grounds 122
Fire Precautions in Places of Public Entertainment and Like
    Premises 123
The Event Safety Guide 126
Legislation 128
Public Entertainment Licensing 129
Security Industry Act 2001 131

8   RISK ASSESSMENT 133
Risk Analysis 135
Pit Teams 137
Risk Documentation 138
Statement of Intent 140

9   "LEAVE YOUR JACKET BEHIND" 143
Attacks and Assaults 145
Kidnap 149
Celebrity Stalking 150
Armed Response 154
The Unusual 157
The SAP 162

10   2007 165

REFERENCES 173

INDEX 181

ACKNOWLEDGEMENTS

Special thanks to my wife Jean and daughters Susan, Linda and Jayne along with my sincere apologies for those times over the years when I was absent. They never questioned the fact that it was just part of the job.

My thanks also to my friend and business partner Gerry Slater for his support and to the many friends and colleagues in the security industry that always supported me. I am also grateful to friends and colleagues from the military who provided excellent training in the early days and friends from the Intelligence Service and the Police for their help and guidance over the years. There are far too many people to mention and they all know who they are.

Last, but by no means least, I would like to thank Professor Chris Kemp and all the team at BCUC (Now Buckinghamshire New University) for guiding me from an army education certificate 3rd class to an Hon Doctorate. It was due entirely to Chris Kemp's encouragement and support that Foundation Degrees in Crowd Safety Management and Protective Security came into being.

FOREWORD

Whenever the name Mick Upton is uttered, it conjures up a mixture of reverence and fondness. Having had the pleasure of knowing Mick for over a decade, and working with him for the last six years, I feel that I have only touched on his enigmatic charm. To see him receive his Honorary Doctorate from the University was one of the highlights of my career. Watching a man who had spent his life in the selfless pursuit of safety at concerts get something back for all of his work was something special and a moment that many people will remember for a long time.

Mick's role as the founder of Showsec, and until 2000 its Chairman, is well known. From a life on the road, where he saw the sharp end of stewarding and crowd management, to engagement as a senior consultant, Mick has been ever-present in the events industry. Using the insight gained from his varied career, he was able to develop a company which believed in education and training as a tool to support the safety of both the audience and the workers at events.

My first meeting with Mick was at a Bon Jovi gig at Milton Keynes Bowl, where a friend of mine said that Mick was just the man to help me in the development of a new event management programme. At the time I was running the Pitz rock club in Milton Keyes, as a promoter and venue manager, and I had just started teaching an events course in my spare time at the local college. When I met Mick, his absolute passion was to start a course that would create a universally recognised pathway through education for those working in the crowd management industry. We talked for ages about this; then I promptly changed jobs, went into education and forgot about our meeting.

However, one day, it dawned on me that it would be good to work at festivals with crowd managers on the Music Industry Management programmes at the then University College. I met up with Mick again and he reminded me of his idea. He then led an epic 18-month course development, assisted by many of those he had managed over the years. This course was the Foundation Degree in Crowd Management and it is still held up as a model in Foundation Degrees across the UK. Without Mick it would not have happened. He continues today assisting with the development of a range of programmes, and I owe all the success of the Crowd Management courses and the founding of the Crowd Management Centre to him.

Mick Upton was our first Head of Centre and opened doors for us which I did not think possible. This book is a testament to Mick's life in the industry and I am sure that you will enjoy reading it as much as I did.

Professor Chris Kemp
November 2007

INTRODUCTION

The branch of the private security industry that is commonly referred to as *leisure security* is actually a diverse web of roles that range from ticket taking at social events to highly complex crowd management operations. In between can be found activities such as door supervision at pubs and clubs, large-scale crowd control operations at sport and a range of social events, the protection of integrity rights (copyright) and celebrity protection. A person that chooses to remain in the industry for a long period of time might well find him/herself working on any or all of these activities.

To cover every avenue of such a diverse industry in any detail would require several books and it is for that reason that I decided to focus on just two strands of this complex industry. As the title suggests this book attempts to trace the origin and development of leisure security as it exists today to serve rock `n` roll and pop music culture. The subjects covered in this review are therefore crowd safety management, crowd control and celebrity protection.

In order to establish the foundations of this leisure security the first chapter provides a brief review of ancient Greek theatre crowd control concepts and a Roman concept of crowd safety by venue design. Chapter two then moves forward to a nineteenth century music hall bouncer culture and on to examine allegations of crowd manipulation in order to create pop stars in the forties. Later chapters then move on to the fifties and the introduction of rock 'n' roll.

I have spent over 50 years working in security environments, starting at the age of 16 as a doorman at a Soho strip club. By the time I was 19 I was a soldier trained in counter terrorist operations. As a 25-year-old civilian I worked freelance on the celebrity protection circuit before joining Artistes Services Ltd where I became head of security and crowd management operations. This company was arguably the first company in the UK to be set up specifically to serve the security needs of event organisers and celebrities. In 1982 I founded what became possibly the largest leisure security company in Europe. That company was ShowSec International Ltd, which I believe was the first company of its type in the UK to set up a residential training school specifically for training in celebrity protection and public safety at events. The diverse range of security scenarios that I have been closely involved in over the years is therefore extensive and

I have tried to pass on my experience by lecturing to civilians, the police service, serving soldiers and government agencies. As much of my time was spent providing a service to concert promoters and celebrities it is inevitable that my research for this book would focus on the security developments that have taken place within musical entertainment.

This book is not an autobiography, however, and there is no scandal! It is intended to be a review of the historical origins of leisure security and the characters that introduced and developed a new security concept to deal with the problems presented by rock 'n' roll. The story is told from personal experience, empirical research data, case study and anecdotal evidence provided by the many friends that I have had the pleasure of working with over the years. Where famous events or people are mentioned it is purely in the interest of illustrating a point. Where I digress into personal anecdotes in Chapter 3 it is simply to explain the influences that steered me toward an industry that has taken me all over the world, allowed me to meet the rich and famous and would see me awarded a Doctorate by Buckinghamshire Chilterns University College for my work on crowd safety and security issues.

My version of the development of an industry is not claimed to be a definitive record. It is simply a personal view and therefore others may view the same industry from a different perspective. In which case I will read their version with interest.

1 THE BEGINNING

A logical place to begin a study of any industry is to consider the earliest documented references to its existence. The leisure security industry that exists in many diverse forms today can trace its origins back over 2000 years to measures that were introduced to control mass crowds at Greek theatre, sport events and Roman games. It is inevitable therefore that a study of the leisure security industry will be a review of the social history of entertainment.

Evidence from ancient venues and sites that still exist indicate by their architectural design that both the ancient Greeks and Romans were aware of the need for good crowd management and crowd control in order to maintain security at massive events. There is ample evidence to support a claim that a spectator culture pre-dates the Roman Empire and its famed chariot races. The modern day Olympic Games are firmly rooted in the events that were staged in ancient Greece prior to the rise of the Roman Empire. The success of games that attracted some 400,000 people indicates that the Athenians had knowledge of the management and control of crowds on a huge scale. The games only took place every four years however, therefore the establishment of Greek theatre was equally important in the development of crowd management theory.

In his excellent published review of Greek theatre, Oliver Taplin (1995) explained that the ancient Greeks had a keen interest in tragic drama, comedy and music and that Athens was the centre of early theatre development. Taplin describes how, in the fourth century BC, a site was prepared in an area above the Temple of Dionysus on the Southwest slope below the Acropolis. At the foot of the site a performance space (the orchestra or dance space), was levelled. The whole area was known as the Theatron (the spectacle, or viewing place). These terms, or adaptations of them, are still used today in venue terminology. It is not possible to establish the exact audience capacity at Dionysus at the time it was built but Taplin suggests that the surviving seats, dated not long before 300 BC indicates an audience capacity of between 14,000 to 20,000 people. Perhaps most importantly in terms of this review, Taplin makes reference to 'officials' who were responsible for orderly conduct – a possible indication that a form of the leisure security industry existed as early as 300 BC.

Taplin's review includes a photographic illustration of a Greek amphitheatre situated at Epidaurus. This photograph clearly demonstrates a venue that was designed to accommodate a large audience with good sight lines, which he argues, was architecturally the finest of many constructed on the Athenian model. Close study of his photograph indicates that the ancient Greeks realised the importance of designing for pedestrian flow, crowd migration and the requirement for an audience to be able to clearly see and hear stage activity. Amphitheatres were constructed in a fan shape in which sound was trapped and carried without echo. Seating consisted of tiered rows of seats that extended from stage to a high level within this fan shape concept. A network of regular entry/exit points and longitudinal and lateral gangways within the auditorium catered for pedestrian movement. There is no record of a major venue crowd related accident at this time therefore it might be reasoned that crowd safety was a consideration in both the venue design and the employment of staff to monitor and control crowd attendance and all pedestrian movements.

Roman entertainment venue planners initially followed the Athenian concept of cutting amphitheatres into hillsides. During 1996 I was invited to visit Israel by the Israeli concert promoters association to assist in the investigation of a fatal accident at a concert held at Arad. During my visit I was invited to see a restored Roman amphitheatre at Caesarea. Built originally by Herod in 10 BC in honour of the Roman Emperor Augustus Caesar, this amphitheatre is regularly used today as a concert venue. The photographs and seating plan shown later illustrate the theatre laid out for a classical concert and entry/exit points, tiered seating and the interior circulation system of the venue. The Athenian influence is clearly demonstrated by the fan shape seating arrangement, longitudinal and lateral pedestrian gangways and entry/egress points. Of particular interest are the entry and egress points which when measured proved to be 1.1 metres in width. This would indicate that the modern day concept of measuring exits in terms of unit widths of a minimum of 550mm is in fact a Roman concept, as it would appear that the current measurement system was commonly used as early as 10 BC.

The photographs and illustrated seating plan indicate that even a small Roman venue would have required a large number of staff to assist people

*Seating plan at the Roman Arena, Caesarea. Nothing has changed since
Roman times.*

A view from stage left of the seating arrangement at Caesarea.

From Ancient Rome to Rock 'n' Roll 15

to their seats and keep order at shows – some that were perhaps not always peaceful in terms of their content. We know from Taplin's research that Greek venues had employed such staff prior to the rise of the Roman Empire.

The Roman discovery of improved building materials, particularly a new form of concrete, allowed them to introduce new construction concepts. No longer restricted to a concept of amphitheatres cut into a hillside, planners were now able to construct multi-level stand-alone buildings. Possibly the best known example of Roman architectural multi-level design for a venue can still be seen today in Rome at the Flavian Amphitheatre, better known as the Colosseum. The Colosseum was constructed during the first century AD. Estimates for capacity of the venue vary between 40,000 to 70,000 people, and these estimates would put the Colosseum in the same category as a UK Premier League football ground or stadium.

In 1996 Robin Brightwell, executive producer of the BBC programme, 'Secrets of Lost Empires', published a review of the Colosseum in which he estimated crowd capacity to be in the region of 45,000 people. Brightwell's research led him to conclude that the whole capacity of the venue could have exited within ten minutes. This would put the venue on a par with safety requirements at contemporary sports grounds. Unfortunately however, Brightwell did not publish his formula for calculating egress flow from the Colosseum.

During 1998 I was able visit the Colosseum and I took the opportunity to test Brightwell's theory. With the help of my son-in-law Mick Sheehan, who studied crowd risk and crisis management at the University of Leicester, we spent three days studying the Roman approach to design for what we would today call a 'complex space'. I set two primary objectives for this study:

1. To discover the extent to which Roman planners had considered crowd safety at the building design stage
2. To gain an insight into the level of staff that would have been necessary to ensure that maximum public safety standards met with venue design.

Specific attention was given to the measurement of ingress, migration and egress facilities; it was reasoned that these were key areas that would have required staff to monitor and ensure public safety standards.

My research project revealed that the venue was designed with a total of 80 entrances/exit gates at ground level. Two of these gates were monumental entrances that lead to central boxes and were for the exclusive use of VIPs. Two other gates were for the use of gladiators and a facility for delivering and removing equipment, and presumably removing the dead, from the arena. This would indicate that there were 76 gates available to the public for ingress and egress. In terms of staff level, the venue design suggests that three categories of staff were needed, as follows:

- VIP protection in the area assigned specifically for the comfort of high profile political guests
- Gladiator preparation and animal area (or backstage) security
- Crowd control necessary when dealing with an audience of possible 60,000 people in terms of containing excitement and ensuring crowd separation or segregation

These three categories remain today at modern venues as the basis for security planning and crowd safety planning.

Public entering the venue required a ticket that indicated the ingress gate that they must use and the location of their seat. The door number system is still visible above some entrances on the north side of the venue. Citizens received free tickets and seat location depending on their social status. Entry gates would lead spectators to a system of four passageways at ground level. These passageways circled the venue inter-linking four quadrants of the building. An obligatory system of stairs in each quadrant then led spectators to their assigned seating level. It was not possible to measure all 76 public entry/exit gates due to the state of the building. Where it was possible to conduct measurements it was found that gates measured 4m in width. Passageways were measured at 5m width and some stairs were found to be 4m wide at their narrowest point.

In order to test Brightwell's egress theory I selected just one quadrant of the venue. The logic applied was that the results obtained could then be multiplied by four in order to achieve a total venue egress time. As the crowd capacity for the venue is open to speculation I decided to use Brightwell's estimate of 45,000 people for my calculation. One quadrant was therefore assumed to hold a capacity of 11,250 people (25% of 45,000). The method used to calculate the final egress test was taken from the formula published in the 1997 fourth edition of the Guide to Safety at Sports Grounds. The Guide states (on page 80) that maximum pedestrian flow from seating accommodation, including gangways, concourses and ramps, can be measured at 73 people per minute per metre of space.

Flow through a final exit can be measured at 109 persons per minute per metre of exit width. Accurate measurement for a flow facility from the stands was not possible due to the state of the building, however building plans provided by the venue indicated that venue design would have accommodated a pedestrian flow of 73 persons. Actual measurement of stairs showed that a flow of 73 persons was possible. With 19 final exits available, and an assumed flow of 109 persons per minute per metre of exit width, support was easily found for Brightwell's estimate of a ten minute evacuation time for the venue. Furthermore, the exit facility available would have easily coped with a capacity far above his estimated capacity of 45,000 people.

This simple test is not claimed here to be scientific evidence. A number of assumptions had been made during calculation regarding active use of the venue, such as width and condition of aisles and gangways, adequate lighting on stairs and orderly crowd behaviour. We can only speculate today on how these variables would affect egress flow. Nevertheless all the indications were that this ancient venue compared favourably with contemporary sports ground design.

It was interesting to compare my findings at the Colosseum with those of the design of Wembley Stadium, London as it was at that time. Wembley Stadium was found to be remarkably similar in design to the Colosseum. An important factor at this point was that the Wembley Stadium employed somewhere in the order of 1000 stewarding staff to control crowds at a major event. This figure was comparable with the figure that I had reached for the Colosseum at the height of its popularity. As the Praetorian Guard would have covered VIP protection and security for restricted areas the level of staff allocated for public areas must be speculation. Nevertheless when consideration is given to a well-established Roman record on issues such as law and civil administration it is perhaps reasonable to assume that an advanced form of the leisure security industry was in being by the first century AD.

If the reader will allow me to digress for a moment, I can reveal one other interesting thing that Mick and I discovered about the Colosseum. During one particularly hot afternoon we decided to return to our hotel roof bar for a beer and as the only people in the bar, we got chatting to the barman. During the course of our conversation he asked us what we were planning to do that evening and we told him that we were intending to

Interior shot of the tiered seating arrangement at the Colosseum in Rome. The VIP area is at the bottom right-hand side of the picture.

return to the Colosseum in the cool of the evening. At this point the barman promptly found work to do and completely ignored us. On our return to the venue later that evening we got chatting to a member of staff who explained that once the tourists had left for the day the area around the venue became a favourite gay meeting place. This apparently happened around 10pm so we made sure we were back in the hotel bar by 9.30pm. Our barman friend obviously got the idea that we were gay and the fact that we had a twin room didn't help. We did try to get a copy of Gay News (or the Italian equivalent) just to

Well-designed ingress and egress system at the Colosseum.

wind up our waiter friend but we couldn't find a copy. The moral to this story for students of venue design is, if you are gay visit after 10pm when it is actually closed and if you are straight make sure you visit during the day and ignore the heat.

To return to our review of the early leisure security industry, there is no way of knowing how well developed the industry was 2000 years ago. We can only search for clues that it did in fact exist. Moving away from the Colosseum to smaller venues, a review of Roman theatre by David Wiles, Reader in Drama at London University, offers us another clue. Wiles (1995) credits the first stone-built auditorium to have been inaugurated by Pompey in 55BC. Wiles explained that Pompey's theatre was a free standing structure, not an excavation into a hillside. Many similar theatres were subsequently built across the Roman world. An interesting observation of this description of Roman theatre by Wiles is that it appears that Emperor Augustus later decreed that Roman audiences should be organised in order to make the auditorium a microcosm of an ordered society. Women, foreigners and serving soldiers were all segregated and male citizens were apparently ordered to wear their togas. It is reasonable to assume that there were people employed specifically to implement these theatre rules. In terms of design, Roman planners moved away from a Grecian style of a separate dance space in favour of one vast stage accommodating the actors and the chorus. The semi-circular orchestra area was then used to seat VIPs. We therefore begin to see the origins of contemporary theatre design and its association with the concept of crowd safety planning. The association of theatre design and crowd management and crowd control presented by Wiles led me to seek examples of Roman influence on contemporary venue design. I was particularly interested in crowd flow organisation and the level of staff necessary to maintain safety standards.

Evidence of Roman influence on modern indoor venue design was easily found at the Royal Albert Hall, London. The management of this prestigious venue provided data to indicate that the basic design for the venue came from civil servant Henry Cole, who travelled round the south of France looking at the ruins of Roman amphitheatres (R.A.H. 1995). The design of the Royal Albert Hall follows the concept of the Colosseum rather than Roman theatre design. The seating plan for 5,200 people is based on a five-tier system incorporating individual seating on the first and fourth levels, private boxes on levels two and three, and standing room on fifth or gallery level. My own observations of the venue established that the ingress, egress, and pedestrian flow around the venue follow the basic principle of the Colosseum.

Visits to other London theatres did however clearly indicate that the Roman concept of a proscenium stage and structured seating plans necessary to afford maximum sight line advantage had been followed. Seating plans and calculations stated in current guidance for pedestrian flow for ingress and egress are therefore based on a theory that originated in first century Rome.

Roman venue planners did not confine their efforts to multi-level buildings and theatres. It is believed that the Hippodrome in Rome was constructed to hold 300,000 spectators to watch chariot racing. This was a huge crowd event even by modern day standards. Unfortunately there is nothing left of the Hippodrome today. The site resembles a large park When you stand on the site however it is possible to imagine the shear scale of the venue and to visualise the problems that the organisers faced in terms of crowd management and control. As there is no record of a major crowd related fatal incident we will never know if these mass crowd events were entirely problem free.

A review of Greco-Roman concepts indicates that good crowd management and crowd control strategies were evident in venue deign over 2000 years ago. To what extent a leisure security industry existed is nevertheless a matter of speculation. There is however one last piece of evidence to point to the fact that the concept of organised crowd control did exist. This final piece of evidence that an organised system of crowd control existed in ancient Rome was also obtained from David Wiles' study of Roman theatre. Wiles provides the text of the prologue to the play Pseudols, written by Plautus and performed in Rome in the year 191 BC. In the prologue spoken to the audience an actor basically list the 'house rules', some of which are as follows:

- The Lictor will keep his words and his whip to himself
- No usher is to block the view or show someone their seat while an actor acts.
- Late-comers, who lingered too long, learn to stand. Or how to get out of bed sooner.
- No slave may sidle in and keep seats free for others.

A *Lictor* is a Roman term for a person that enforces rules, and the term has been used to refer to magistrate officers and bodyguards. For example, in his book *The Dream of Rome*, Boris Johnson (2006) states that Caesar was provided with 72 Lictors when referring to bodyguards. The use of the term 'usher' is interesting in that it is the common term used in America today for the person referred to in the UK as a steward.

For the student of leisure security therefore the logical start point for a journey of discovery is the lessons of history. We have seen that 'officials' were on hand at Greek amphitheatres and Lictors at Roman venues to maintain public order. Ancient event promoters incorporated what we now call 'leisure security' to deal with the psychology of a mass crowd as early as 300BC, demonstrating that crowd control was a well-established concept. Equally important are ancient concepts of venue design, which still serve today to underpin our approach to crowd safety management and emergency evacuation.

2 FROM MUSIC HALL TO ROCK 'N' ROLL

Music Hall might be considered by many people to be an unlikely subject to include in a review of the leisure security industry. The decision to make a quantum leap from Roman events to music hall is made in this chapter because the period of music hall popularity produced the first artistes that would become international pop stars. Pop and rock culture would subsequently provide a huge client base for a contemporary leisure security industry. By following the natural development of this form of entertainment we will eventually reach areas of leisure security that include concert crowd control, door supervision and celebrity protection.

Michael Booth, Chair of the Department of Theatre at the University of Victoria, British Columbia, has explained that music hall was a form of social entertainment that evolved to satisfy a working class need for an entertainment form that was light-hearted and not bound by theatre etiquette. In his informative work on this form of entertainment, Booth (1995) explained that at the early stages of development the prime function of these venues was to sell food and drink. Entertainment was provided as an incentive to attract customers to what was basically a bar. Booth describes how a chairman would announce the artistes and keep order, no doubt assisted by staff who would throw out drunks who overstepped such rules that might have existed.

An interesting feature of nineteenth century music hall was the parallel course developed in the United States of America. Exactly why it was that two countries separated by such a vast distance should both ignore other European influences and choose to adopt allied cultures is open to speculation. One possibility is simply the fact that the two countries shared a common language. Whatever the reason, both countries have subsequently proved to be a major influence in the development of modern day cultures such as pop and rock music, both of which can trace their roots back to music hall. The American form of music hall was referred to as vaudeville. Booth reveals that American vaudeville, like its British counterpart, grew out of beer halls, principally in the western United

States where it answered a desperate need for light entertainment amongst audiences of miners, lumbermen, cowboys, and gunfighters.

There does not appear to be any hard evidence that security teams were employed at venues during this period. There is however ample evidence to indicate that public disorder was not uncommon in theatre venues. A riot is recorded as early as 1762 at the Covent Garden Theatre, London, when an attempt was made to increase ticket prices. Other incidents include riots due to the introduction of foreign artistes at the Haymarket Theatre, London in 1779 and similar incidents occurred in 1809 and 1848. Given the fact that music hall emerged and flourished during this period it is perhaps not unreasonable to speculate that theatre operators would have hired local hard men to deal with crowd problems. What we now call 'Door Supervisors' in the UK were then called bouncers, so called because they would quickly bounce a person out of the venue if they misbehaved. It is likely that employing bouncers was a well-established practice in nineteenth century taverns and drinking clubs.

From a crowd safety perspective the development of nineteenth century popular entertainment venues was not conducted without serious crowd safety problems. Possibly the highest risk to public safety at these venues was that of fire due to the inflammable materials used within the building and for scenery. It is worth pausing to consider some of these serious incidents and the influence that they would have had in developing training systems for a largely unorganised leisure security industry.

In America a terrible fire at the Brooklyn Theatre, New York, in 1876 caused the death of 283 people. Seven years after the Brooklyn Theatre fire it appears that American architects thought that they had overcome the problem of theatre fires when they announced that the newly-built Iroquois Theatre, Chicago, to be immune from fire. The Iroquois advertised that it was 'absolutely fireproof', and this claim appears to be based on the fact that a sprinkler system had been installed and the building had electric lighting. Unfortunately however, the theatre burnt down on 30th December 1903, just six weeks after it had opened. In her research into the cause and effect of the fire, Joyce Robins (1992) revealed that there were no fire extinguishers available, no fire alarms and the sprinkler system was not in working order. There were 30 exits but most of them appeared to be locked as a security precaution and the theatre was allegedly overcrowded. Robins estimates that the theatre had 1,600 seats but there were nearer 2,000 people packed inside with hundreds standing in the gangways. Six-hundred-and-two people died in the fire which started on the stage and quickly spread, causing thick smoke to the upper levels of the theatre. The death total in this 'fire proof' theatre was double that of the Brooklyn Theatre 27 years earlier! The problem of overcrowding and locked exits as a part of security measures was to be an ongoing problem that still exists today.

There were serious theatre fires throughout Europe during the nineteenth century. Major fires occurred in Paris and Vienna and in the UK there was a very serious one at the Theatre Royal, Exeter, in 1887 that claimed the lives of 186 people (see *The Exeter Theatre Fire* by David Anderson, also published by Entertainment Technology Press). Fire risk became such a serious problem that strong action was needed to make theatres safer and in 1880 a Captain Shaw of the London Fire Brigade launched an intensive study of London theatre safety. Following his report safety at theatres was improved but fire risk was not eliminated. On the 9th May 1911 an illusionist at the Empire Palace Theatre, Edinburgh, accidentally set fire to the stage during his act and nine members of the stage crew and the illusionist died in the fire. The interesting thing about this fire is that all the 3000 members of the audience escaped unharmed within 2.5 minutes. The time factor is explained by a popular story that the stage safety curtain was lowered and the orchestra played the National Anthem, which apparently took 2.5 minutes. Subsequently 2.5 minutes became the maximum escape time for all public venues in the UK until venue construction improvements were introduced. There are now variations of escape time according to venue construction. For the moment it is important to stress that the escape time set by the Edinburgh fire of 1911 formed the basis for constructing training programmes for venue managers and staff with regard to emergency evacuation.

Escape from a fire was not the only reason for considering how an emergency evacuation needed to be carefully planned. Natural laws of crowd dynamics dictate that peaceful crowd gatherings can build up tremendous pressure loads if the crowd is not effectively managed and controlled. One of the worst crowd related incidents recorded in the UK was at the Victoria Hall Theatre, Sunderland, on Saturday 16th June 1883. On that afternoon the theatre was showing a special children's variety show. It is estimated that over 1000 children were seated in the gallery level. At the end of the performance it was announced that any child that held a ticket marked with a particular number would receive a prize as they left the theatre. In the rush down stairs that followed this announcement 183 children were killed in a crowd collapse. Data provided by the Cabinet Office Emergency Planning College (EPC) indicates that, prior to the Victoria Hall tragedy crowd crush incidents in theatres occurred with frightening regularity, for example:

> 1849: 70 people died in an egress incident at a Glasgow theatre
>
> 1853: six people were killed at the Surrey Gardens Music Hall in what is recorded as a crowd surge
>
> 1858: 15 people were killed in a crowd surge at the Royal Victoria Theatre (now the Old Vic)
>
> 1868: 23 people died at Langs Victoria Music Hall in an egress crush.

In spite of horrific incidents that occurred at theatres at the time the best known artistes of the period played to capacity houses. What began as local entertainment in taverns had evolved to become an entertainment business. Soon the best known artistes were travelling abroad, and at this point variety and vaudeville had evolved to become a profitable international entertainment business.

An important feature of music hall and vaudeville entertainment were song and dance acts that would encourage an audience to sing along. Often the lyrics to a new song would be projected on to a screen for the audience to follow, and song publishing became big business. In the middle to late 1800s and early 1900s, the sale of sheet music, which could be purchased from local shops or street corner vendors, was the major source of revenue for the publisher.

For music publishers to ensure that their latest product reached the ears of the most popular performers of the time it was necessary to employ the services of a song plugger. These people, in many cases it would be the composer, would use any means at their disposal to get a popular artiste to listen to, and hopefully include, this latest song in their stage act. Today the song plugger would be known as a record plugger, a person hired by record companies to ensure that records and videos are played on radio and TV stations.

Eventually theatre and music hall would split into two distinctly separate cultures. Traditional theatres continued to present drama while music halls became known as a 'palace of varieties'. Subsequently this descriptive term was shortened and they would be referred to commonly as 'variety theatres'. As a young boy growing up in Camden Town, North London, during the forties, I was fortunate enough to experience the tail end of Music Hall as it transformed to become variety. On a Friday night a gang of us would 'bunk in' by creeping in a side exit door of the Bedford Theatre which had been a traditional Music Hall but it now presented a mix of traditional Music Hall acts and variety artistes.

At the Bedford we would open an exit and make what seemed to us to be like a climb up the north face of Everest. In fact it was a trek up the stone stairs until we reached the gallery – every step taken with extreme caution in case we were caught. On reaching the gallery we would sit on stone steps similar to a Roman amphitheatre design. The gallery was an exciting place to be as a kid; people would shout abuse at acts that had failed to entertain and it was known for people to throw things at the stage to encourage an act to get off! There were many occasions when I saw bouncers deliver a smack round the ear to someone in the gallery that had been judged to have 'broken house rules', although nobody was ever sure what the house rules were.

To us young lads the most 'must see' act at the Bedford was 'Jane of the Daily Mirror'. Jane had been a cartoon pin-up character for the troops during World War II and after the war an enterprising promoter had the idea of touring Jane as a nude show. In hindsight there were probably a number of Jane's touring the country at the same time. We were convinced that we were seeing the real thing however. In reality Jane (or whatever her real name was) appeared nude on a raised platform and posed for a couple of minutes with a curtain strategically covering her vital parts. By today's standards of course this act would be laughed off the stage. It was argued by the well informed at the time that Jane actually wore a body stocking but to a bunch of 12-year-old boys however this was the height of eroticism that could be savoured and exaggerated to all our friends. Whenever Jane appeared at the Bedford we were sure to be at the front of the gallery.

My mother was quite a keen variety theatre fan although as an office cleaner she could rarely afford to go. My dad had returned from a German prisoner of war camp in 1945 and took up employment as a lorry driver but, like a lot of men of his generation, he spent most of his money in the local pub. He did enjoy music, he had taught himself to play the piano and the accordion, which enabled to him to earn extra cash plying in the pub and on the coach during pub summer outings. We never saw this extra cash in the home however. On the rare occasions that my mother could afford it, such as a birthday or Christmas treat, she would take me to the Finsbury Park Empire which always presented the big acts of day. On one memorable occasion she took me to the London Palladium where I saw the famous comedian Sid Fields. I have to confess that as a 12-year-old I didn't understand too much of the humour; it was only years later when I saw film of his sketches that I understood! Nevertheless the theatre was a magical place and looking back now on those years it is easy to see that theatre visits were the influences that would later in life steer me toward working in the entertainment industry.

While the sub culture of variety theatres had eliminated the need for a 'chairman' to introduce acts and keep order, it did continue a tradition of encouraging audience participation. It was in variety theatres that artistes also discovered the importance of stage lighting techniques and the importance of good sound systems to their act. Variety existed as a form of popular entertainment until the 1950s when the introduction of television as a mass entertainment medium encouraged people to stay at home to be entertained. Variety theatre culture had virtually disappeared by the sixties.

By the mid-twentieth century new technology in the form of sound recording had made it possible to record the singing voice and add dialogue to silent motion pictures. A short time later radio became freely available. The most talented artistes of this period naturally took advantage of this new technology to achieve greater international fame. Sound recordings become a sales factor in 1930 and the first charts published to indicate the sale of a combination of sheet music and recordings was published in 1935 in America. Charts to indicate the sale of recordings alone originated in the American magazine Billboard in July 1940. Britain's first record chart appeared in New Musical Express 12 years later, in November 1952.

Arguably the first popular singer to have taken full advantage of new recording technology was the American vaudeville artiste Al Jolson who was the first artiste to sell one million copies of a pop record. Murrells (1974) *Book of Golden Discs'*, lists 'Ragging the Baby to Sleep' by Al Jolson to have been released on the Victor label on the 12th April 1912 in

America. This record by a popular (later shortened to pop) singer could perhaps be classified as the origins of pop culture, as we know it today.

It was inevitable that Jolson's success would alert others to the sales potential of popular music in the form of recordings. New recording companies were set up and new talent found to record. By the end of the thirties recording and marketing popular songs was a big international business. The early 1940s saw records made by male singers marketed in a very positive way. Unlike movie heroes of the period, who were inaccessible, this new breed of recording hero was marketed as 'the boy next door'.

There is no hard evidence to show that recording company executives took a deliberate decision to target adolescent females in a sales campaign, however there are indications to suggest that they did do so. Young women were deliberately led to believe that radio stars were available romantically. An early indication of this policy is seen by the campaign to market Frank Sinatra. The singer first came to prominence by singing on radio programmes with big bands that were popular during the period. His timing, phrasing, and interpretation of a romantic lyric were quickly recognised by recording executives as good sales potential. To enhance his reputation it became common practice to announce him on radio as, *'the voice'*.

In an article, published in the *Daily Mail* under the title, 'Sinatra the Man', K. Kelly (1998), alleged that young women were paid by publicist George Evans to scream hysterically at the singer during live radio broadcasts. In their review of pop music culture for the period Hanif Kureishi and Jon Savage (1995) also alleged that Evans was responsible for paying fans to scream at Sinatra and of manipulating the media. It is a fact that stories aimed at young women were continually planted in the press. These stories would describe the singer's taste in cloths, in cars, and his lifestyle. Evans was also thought to have been behind the creation of a descriptive term for Sinatra fans. The term *'bobby soxers'*, used to describe Sinatra fans was a reference to the short ankle length socks commonly worn by young women at that time.

The degree of success achieved by this marketing strategy can be seen in an account published by Bruce Blivin under the title 'The Voice and the Kids'. Blivin describes how 10,000 young women tried to get into a Sinatra concert at the Paramount Theatre, New York, in 1944. The theatre capacity was only 3,500 and an estimated 150 police officers failed to keep order among disappointed fans outside. Some people had apparently queued all night and others tried to buy a place near the front of the queue. One parent reported that his daughter had threatened to kill herself if she was prevented from trying to going to the concert and those that were unsuccessful in getting a ticket are alleged to have caused widespread damage to property nearby. When considered in detail this account is likely to be highly exaggerated. For example it is extremely unlikely that the NYPD could have detailed 150 police officers to attend the event but it made great publicity. From this point on the singer would be provided with police protection whenever he appeared in public and his press agent would have been very satisfied with a job well done.

America circa 1944 would therefore appear to locate both the place and time that mass crowd hysteria at concert events began. For as Simon Frith observed in his book, "Sound Effects: Youth, Leisure and the Politics of Rock 'n' Roll", *"at this point the technology of mass media communication had changed the relationship of the masses to art"*. Creation had become a collective, rather than an individual process. In the mid 1950s popular music in the UK existed in two broad categories – pop and rock 'n' roll – and both were dominated by American influence. Pop singers sang mainly with big bands and their promotion, followed in the Sinatra tradition.

During the early fifties audience hysteria was a well-known phenomenon at pop concerts in the USA and the UK. In the UK popular band singers such as Dickie Valentine, who sang with the Ted Heath Band, took advantage of the situation by moving away from big bands to perform solo at theatres in order to enhance their career and a British pop market was created. Dickie Valantine came from my neighbourhood, and although I cannot claim that he was a friend of mine, he was actually seven or eight years older than I was and as a teenager he would have rightly considered me to be a kid. I can claim however to have been at what may have been his singing debut in a talent contest at the Forum Cinema Kentish Town (now a live music venue).

Dickie's father was a foreman at the Kentish Town depot of General Roadways (later British Road Services – Islington Group) where my dad was employed as a driver. I spent many hours at the depot filling the trucks with diesel or helping to load/unload vehicles, and the drivers would always give me a shilling or two for helping out.

Tragically, Dickie Valantine was killed in a car crash in 1971. Some years later I was working as Head of Security and Crowd Safety on a live outside broadcast programme for the BBC and I was surprised to meet a stage manager who was the spitting image of Dickie Valantine as I remembered him when I was a boy. It turned out that the stage manager was Dickie Valantine's son, Richard Valantine. I enjoyed a conversation with Richard about his dad and his grandfather who it turned out was now in his eighties. The next time Richard and I met he told that he had recently seen his grandfather and he still remembered me as a cheeky kid that was always bunking off school to earn a few bob at his depot and he had difficulty coming to terms with the fact that I was now a 6' 4" Head of Security. Young Richard, as I call him, is, at the time of writing, a BBC TV director.

The birth of what we now call rock music arguably began in an area of the city of New Orleans known as 'The French Quarter'. In 1897 this area was defined within 38 blocks of the Storyvill district, known also as the 'District'. Within this area flourished brothels, gambling joints, saloons, dives and cabaret clubs (Keepnews & Grauer 1955). It was against this backdrop that musicians worked and developed their talents in numerous cultural directions. It is not unreasonable to assume that these musicians would also have come into daily contact with security staff or bouncers at these establishments, thus continuing between entertainment venues and a security industry, albeit a very loose industry.

In his 1992 book, *American Rock 'n' Roll Tour,* Dave Walker identified American disc jockey Alan Freed as being an influential figure in introducing a change of crowd attitudes by the introduction of black rhythm and blues (R&B) artistes to white American audiences. Walker explains that Freed was advised by a record shop owner named Leo Mintz in 1951 that white record buyers were developing an interest in what was still referred to as race music. At this time Freed was working with radio station WJW in Cleveland Ohio and he introduced R&B music into his programme, and it became immensely popular with younger listeners. During 1954 Freed was invited to join station WINS in New York where he continued to play what was still R&B to a growing audience of teenagers. By this time Freed had titled his radio programme *Moondogs Rock and Roll Party* and here we see the possibly the first popular use of the term rock 'n' roll.

Freed used his radio programme to successfully launch a second career as a promoter of live rock 'n' roll concerts and it is from this point on that we begin to see references to crowd violence at rock concerts. On March 21, 1952, Freed promoted the Moondog Coronation Ball at the Cleveland Arena, Cleveland, Ohio, an event that is now regarded by many people to have been the first event promoted as a rock 'n' roll concert. Unfortunately, most references to the event also refer to a riot caused by gross overcrowding, gate crashing and fights between security staff and non-ticket holders.

Freed was again involved in a crowd related incident when he promoted a rock 'n' roll show at the Boston Arena in May 1958. Accounts of this particular event allege that there was serious crowd trouble outside the venue and that several girls were raped. Inside the venue it appears that a white woman jumped onto the stage and grabbed the crotch of a black singer which then caused the crowd to riot. There are also reports which claim that prejudiced white police officers objected to black artistes performing to a non-segregated audience. Freed was apparently arrested for inciting a riot, the rest of the tour was cancelled, and he returned to New York where he was fired by Radio Station WINS.

A reputation for crowd problems at rock 'n' roll concerts spread even further when Bill Haley established himself as a leading exponent of the culture. Haley released his first record 'Rock the Joint' in 1952, but it was not until a year later when he released his second record 'Crazy Man Crazy ' that he achieved success. This second record sold a million copies. Then came the record that was to establish him as a leading influence on fifties rock culture. 'Rock Around the Clock' had originally been made as a single record release in 1954 but its chart success owed much to the fact that it was also the sound track for the film Blackboard Jungle a year later. The 1974 edition of Murrells Book of Golden Discs indicates that Rock Around the Clock sold one million records in the USA in 1955 and it remained at number one in the American national charts for seven weeks. Apart from the huge American sales, it went on to become the first record to sell over one million copies in Britain where it remained at number one in the UK charts for five weeks.

The impact of Haley's rock 'n' roll on Britain in 1955 was extraordinary. It was a time when the country was only just recovering from the full impact of World War II and the county's youth were struggling to establish their own identity. Britain's leading youth cult of the decade was the 'Teddy Boy', or 'Edwardian' look. In his 1978 study of fifties youth culture Peter Lewis describes the culture as: *"Urban working class boys who sought an identity through draped jackets, velvet collars and drainpipe trousers. They pursued violent gang warfare and vandalism in the streets and dance halls"*. Teddy Boy culture eagerly accepted Haley's brand of rock 'n' roll which Lewis describes a *'youthquake'*, a reference to the fact that post war youth had, for the first time, money to spend on leisure. A newly found independence had created conditions which allowed a new youth culture to reject standards that had been set by an earlier generation in favour of enjoying their own style of music, fashion and film.

From its very beginning this new music style was regarded by an older generation that had survived the horror of World War II to be a non-conformist ideology aimed solely at youth. The association of Bill Haley with crowd disorder was never far from the news in fifties. For example, a Daily Telegraph report of September 1956 was typical:

"Police were called to five cinemas in London and surrounding districts last night to deal with excited young people creating disturbances during the film Rock Around the Clock *... Teddy Boys and girls started by clapping hands and banging their feet to the rhythm of the music. As the tempo grew faster they left their seats to dance in the gangways."*

Although Bill Haley was undoubtedly influential in the initial establishment of fifties rock 'n' roll culture his influence only appears to have been portrayed on his recordings. His first live concert performance in Great Britain was at the Dominion Theatre, London, on February 6th 1957. Although the house was sold out, it only amounted to 3,000 people. This would appear to be a rather small-scale debut for an artiste who had established an international reputation for causing mass crowd problems. The Daily Telegraph report of the Dominion show notes that the audience *"cheered, sang, clapped in time with the music, and showed nothing more harmful than healthy enthusiasm"*. My own experience of Haley, gained as his personal protector during a short 'come-back' tour of England during the seventies was that he lacked the stage presence necessary for a major act, in fact much of the stage presentation was left to members of his band, The Comets. Admittedly this was some 16 years after his debut. In reality however it was the emergence of Elvis Presley that provided a highly commercial image to rock 'n' roll.

In their review of 25 years of rock, John Tobler and Pete Frame (1993) reveal that Presley's first record for the RCA label was *Heartbreak Hotel*, issued in 1956, and by March that year it was number one in all US charts. The promotion of Elvis Presley was undoubtedly a masterpiece of marketing that was reminiscent of the earlier campaign to launch Frank Sinatra. No promotional campaign could reach the level of success achieved by both Sinatra and Presley however unless the artiste has a considerable amount of talent and both certainly had plenty of that. Early promotional tactics did however rely much on personal image and the uses of a christen name or title. Where Sinatra was billed as 'Frankie' or 'the voice', Presley was billed as 'Elvis' or 'the King'. Reporting on Presley's 1956 American concert tour, the Daily Mirror reporter Donald Craine wrote:

"I have just escaped from a hurricane called Elvis Presley.
A few hints of what this tall, rangy singer is doing to young America with his rock-'n'-roll rhythm had already reached me.

- *In Jacksonville, Florida, he had to be rescued from a crowd in a police wagon.*
- *In Wichita Falls, Texas, the fans broke every window of his car.*
- *In San Diego, California, a pack of teenage girls had covered his windscreen with phone numbers written in lipstick...*

I saw him send 5,000 of them (young women*) into a mass fit of screaming hysterics."* (Craine: Daily Mirror: 30th April 1956.)

Craine's report is interesting in as much as it does not simply report the reaction of the audience, it virtually publishes a list of actions that adolescent females should indulge in. Craine therefore followed a marketing trend set earlier by Evans for Frank Sinatra.

Today Elvis is still remembered by his fans as simply 'the King'. In the early stage of his career Elvis appealed to an audience of mainly young women who would reacted hysterically to his stage performance and he set a trend for a pop rock style that was quickly copied by a great many imitators.

An important American artiste that was responsible for spreading crowd hysteria in pop culture was Johnnie Ray, and crowd hysteria was a regular feature of his concerts. In a review of a his concert at the London Palladium in May 1955, Sunday Pictorial reporter Bernard McElwaine raised the question: *"Is Johnnie Ray – the singer who flays audiences of 2,000 at a time with an emotional hot live wire – a mass hypnotist?"* McElwaine describes how he took an unnamed doctor to the concert in order to gain a medical opinion on the hysterical reaction by the audience to the singer's performance. The doctor's observations were claimed to be 'startling'. He (the doctor), apparently waved his hand in front of a girl's face and she was unconscious of what he was doing. This apparently led the doctor to conclude that when a person uses a form of communication, which is not directed to the intelligence – and when this communication produces uncontrolled physical effects – then that is mass hypnotism.

McElwaine's research can hardly be described as a scientific experiment, and it would seem more likely that his report was actually another example of media complicity in marketing a performer. Nevertheless the reporter drew on an important mass hypnosis theory that has its roots in nineteenth century theoretical concepts to underpin his story. Mass crowd hypnosis, or crowd single mind, is a very important consideration in training programmes for leisure security staff today.

By the end of the fifties this new pop rock style was firmly established in the UK. National television shows such as 'Six-Five Special' and 'Oh Boy', had ensured that rock was no longer exclusive to Teddy Boys and audience profile at concerts was predominantly young females. A new breed of British rock artiste had emerged with macho names like Marty Wilde and Billy Fury. These acts followed the Elvis Presley concept of rock in that they used the combination of rock 'n' roll dynamics and pop presentation. Artistes would tour the country together in a bus stopping to play at theatres, town halls and even swimming baths that would cover a pool for the night. Session musicians would normally accompany these artistes, and it was possibly the arrival of Cliff Richard and The Shadows that introduced a group as an act rather than focusing on a solo singer concept.

Cliff Richard entered the UK national charts with *'Please Don't Tease'* in 1960 and his backing group The Shadows entered the charts at the same year with *'Apache'*. Audience profile for Cliff's concerts was, and still is, predominately female. There was a fundamental difference between pop and rock at this stage. Pop was clearly defined for listening to. Dance halls catered for the needs of dancers. Usually referred to as *ballrooms*, dance halls revelled in names such the Mayfair, Roxy or Lacarno. At the end of the forties and beginning of the fifties they catered for a sedate form of dancing, and these venues were places that people went to meet members of the opposite sex. Many a wedding was the end result of a chance meeting at the local Palais de Dance on a Friday or Saturday night. The objective of dance halls was for couples to embrace each other while dancing to a waltz played by a strict tempo orchestra and bouncers quickly dealt with any form of rowdy behaviour.

By the late fifties couples no longer wanted to dance clutching each other. Ultimately they would not want to dance together at all – they would be quite content to simply gyrate on the dance floor without a partner. It was possibly the alarming cost of replacing damaged seats at theatres that prompted concert promoters to move their rock concerts to ballrooms and unseated venues. For the concert promoter dance halls were a logical place to present their acts because young people had the freedom of space that they were looking for to dance how they wanted to and they had the added benefit of in-house of security staff able to deal with unacceptable behaviour.

The emergence of the Beatles in 1962 caused a major shift in crowd attitudes. Audiences at their concerts were not a real problem inside a theatre, it was outside that there were major crowd problems. The group was initially influenced by R&B but they quickly demonstrated a talent for writing and in 1963 the Beatles regularly topped the UK charts. Their first album *'Please Please Me'* topped the album charts for 30 weeks. By 1964 Beatle mania was a worldwide phenomena and public appearances attracted huge crowds that required a large police presence to ensure crowd control.

It would be the emergence of the Rolling Stones however that caused a shift in crowd behaviour from hysteria to a high-energy release and even violence. Working with the Stones in 1984/65 I regularly witnessed audiences going absolutely crazy during performances. People jumping onto the stage to touch the group became a major problem that required a line of security staff to be placed in front of the stage for protection but this was not always successful. Band member Keith Richard graphically described this period as follows:

"There was a period in England when we couldn't play ballrooms any more because we never got through more than three or four songs every night, man. Chaos. Police and too many people in the places, fainting. We'd walk into some of those places and it was like they had the Battle of the Crimea going on, people gasping, tits hanging out, chicks choking, nurses running around with ambulances".

(Richard K: 1981)

It was clear by the end of the sixties that what had began as a nineteenth century musical hall attempt to satisfy a working class need for light-hearted entertainment had diversified to become an international entertainment industry. The arrival of rock 'n' roll subsequently caused a change in youth cultural behaviour that traditional venue management procedure failed to control. Venues initially tried to use dance hall bouncers to exert control in the form of preventing stage invasions but this was bound to fail. What was needed was a whole new approach to crowd safety management at concert events, but it would be a long time yet before venues and promoters fully realised that crowd safety management is a social science.

3 LONDON TO LOS ANGELES

This chapter is intended to illustrate the influences that steered me toward the leisure security career path that my life has followed over the years. It is a path that took me from a house in Camden Town, North London, to mix with the rich and famous in Los Angeles and many other exotic places around the world. I hope I will be forgiven for what might appear to be a self-indulgent chapter; it is not intended to inflate my ego.

I was two years old when World War II started and, like a great many other London kids in the war, I found myself evacuated by the age of five. I was sent to Cheshire where I was billeted along with three others with a village policeman and his family. I was ungrateful for their hospitality however and I ran away three times. After the third time I was put into a home from which I promptly ran away again. The root of my problem was that, in spite of the air raids I missed London and I hated being surrounded by green fields.

Finally the authorities got fed up with this cockney pest and I was sent home. On arriving back in London I was surprised to find several others had also been sent home and that schools were closed due to the bombing. It was a period when we spent most of our time pestering American soldiers for chewing gum and chocolate. This seemed like a perfect situation to us kids. The down-side of course was that we missed out on our education but we did not realise that for some years.

The post-war Camden Town of my childhood was an area filled with plenty of bombed sites that provided exciting, albeit dangerous, play areas. Delivery and collection services such as the milkman, coalman and dustbin men all drove horse and carts. Only Camden High Street seemed to have vehicles in the form of trams that clattered up and down. Our house had a yard with an outside toilet, a tin bath and gas lighting. The only time that I saw electric lighting was in shops. I was 12 before I realised that some people actually had electric light in their house. Consequently my home entertainment consisted of listening to a wireless that was powered by an accumulator that had to be charged every week. It was my job to take the accumulator to a shop in Royal

College Street where it would be exchanged for a fully charged one for a fee of sixpence (2.5p).

With a fully charged accumulator it was possible to listen to Dick Barton Special Agent each weeknight at 6:45pm on the BBC Light Programme. With his faithful companions Jock and Snowy, Dick Barton managed to get himself into a life-threatening situation every night. Another 'must listen to' wireless programme was on every Sunday at midday. Two-Way Family Favourites played record requests and sent messages to the troops stationed abroad and it was the nearest the dear old BBC came to playing pop records at that time. On one occasion when I was sick my mother made up a bed for me downstairs in the kitchen and I was allowed to listen to the wireless because I could not sleep. It was on this occasion that I heard the trumpet legend Kenny Baker and I was immediately hooked on jazz. From then on I would stay up every Thursday night to listen to the Kenny Baker Dozen and I would discover that these musicians were hand picked professionals who also played with many of the famous big bands of the day.

Reflecting on the influences that were powerful in my life I have come to the conclusion that it was always inevitable that I would end up working in the leisure security industry. On the one hand there was my excitement at visits to the theatre and a keen interest in jazz music. Another important influence on me as a child was the sport of boxing. Like a lot of kids brought up in post war Britain I joined a boxing club. My first boxing coach was a man by the name of Charlie Webster, an old pro who came from a highly respected boxing family and who had a very effective tuition style. Having impressed upon me before I entered the ring the importance of always keeping my guard up, he promptly delivered a left hook to my chin in the first round! I had of course let my guard slip down. Charlie no doubt considered the blow to be a 'tap', to me it felt like a thunderbolt. In those days clubs could not afford head guards and anyone that trained to box at that time will vividly remember the first time that they received a punch.

At this point I must emphasise that Charlie Webster was *not* some kind of sadistic bully. What I perhaps did not appreciate then was that he was teaching me a very valuable lesson. In a conflict situation the two most important things to remember are to manage your fear and control your aggression. Once I realised that being punched in the face was not actually as devastating as I had imagined it would be I was able to think about coming forward to deliver blows in a controlled fashion. Six years later I would discover that military instructors at Aldershot would use the same technique on their new recruits only they called it 'milling', a situation where an instructor would pick out two people that had to demonstrate controlled aggression during boxing. Taking part was mandatory for every member of the squad and we were warned in advance that any person that was considered guilty of not giving 100% commitment would have to box the instructor. We were told that the aim of the exercise was to demonstrate controlled aggression, which was what Charlie Webster had done.

I boxed from the age of 12 until the age of 16, but stopped following a spell in hospital. On the Friday before Christmas 1953 I was due to attend a Christmas dance and I decided to have my hair cut at Carlo's barbershop opposite my house. I sat in the chair and just as Carlo started to cut my hair I collapsed. The barber knew me well and he quickly got me across the road to my home with the help of other customers. My mother immediately went two doors down the street to our doctor. On examining me, Doctor Kessle immediately called an ambulance. I had peritonitis (burst appendix). I can still remember being in an ambulance with a bell ringing – they did not use sirens in those days – but the rest is a blur. When I eventually regained consciousness I found myself in the Middlesex Hospital in Mortimer Street where I remained over Christmas. My condition must have been serious because I was in the Middlesex Hospital for several weeks. During the last week of January 1954 I was transferred to a convalescent home at Clacton on Sea in order to recuperate from my operation. Unfortunately, shortly after my arrival at Clacton the East Coast of England experienced the worst storms ever on the night of January 31st and the sea front area and part of the town suffered serious flooding. The floods were so bad along the coast that the emergency services were badly stretched and volunteers were called for to move people from flooded areas to dry land. Consequently I found my self rowing a small boat up and down streets ferrying people to the Roaring Donkey pub where the landlord and staff did a magnificent job providing food and drinks to one and all.

I returned to London from Clacton in February and to work at a local cigarette factory where I met Jean, who would become my wife, in 1955. Prior to meeting her however, a neighbour of mine, who happened to work in a Soho club, arranged for me to start work as a doorman at a strip club in Wardour Street just before my seventeenth birthday. I was paid the princely sum of £5 per night, which meant that working three nights was the equivalent of treble the wage I was earning at the factory. At this time the clubs in Soho were controlled by what today would be called organised crime. Everyone knew this and very few people were willing to take on the gangsters who ran the area. All that was required in terms of club door work was for a big guy who could handle himself to keep an eye on things. At 6' 4" with an ability to throw a punch correctly I fitted the bill. If serious trouble was threatened the woman in the ticket booth was instructed to immediately phone a given number and the cavalry would arrive armed with all sorts of weaponry. On their arrival I was instructed to stand aside and let them deal with the problem.

Given the fact that a person had to be 21 years of age to go into a strip club in those days I was actually too young to be in there! Nobody asked my age when I started or during the period that I worked there however. It appeared that age was not of interest and things went well for a couple of weeks. That is until the night a group of Royal Navy sailors decided to visit the club. I should have known better than to let in a bunch of drunken sailors but to a green teenager they were a bunch of big spenders and I had been instructed *never* to turn away potential big spenders. The navy paid their money and made their way up the stairs to the dimly lit club, which was actually a small room with chairs set out in rows with a small stage at one end. The stage could perhaps be more accurately described as a platform about eighteen inches high with plastic flowers around the edge.

About 20 minutes after the navy had entered the club I heard a terrific scream from upstairs. The women in the pay booth grabbed the phone and I rushed up the stairs to find one hysterical stripper and the cream of the British Navy in fits of laughter. It turned out that during her act the stripper turned her back to her audience and bent over and at this point an artistically minded sailor plucked a plastic daffodil from the front of the stage and pushed it up her rear! The stripper was now demanding that I give the navy a good hiding, which did not seem like a great idea to me at all. I knew that some very heavy guys were at this moment rushing down Old Compton Street to deal out instant justice in the form of cracked heads, and this could end up as total chaos and I would be in the middle of it. I did the only thing that I could think of, and shouted as loud as I could that the Shore Patrol was on their way.

It was common practice at this time for the military police to patrol Soho and the shore patrol was the Royal Navy version of the military police and they had a reputation for cracking heads without asking questions. On hearing that the patrol was on its way the club emptied in seconds. The cavalry arrived to find the navy rushing past them out into the street. Upstairs they found an empty club and they were astonished by the fact that I had thrown out a contingent of the Mediterranean Fleet single-handed. I of course never mentioned how I had done it, preferring to let them believe that the navy had run off rather than face me. I was enjoying basking in my new-found glory of the single-handed defeat of the navy when the club manager arrived. On finding the club empty he nearly had a fit – I had got rid of all of the potential big spenders. He was not a bit interested in the indignant stripper or my recently acquired fearsome reputation. He sacked me on the spot. My first job in the private security industry had lasted a mere three weeks.

I was not unduly worried about my loss of employment. I had given up boxing following my stay in hospital and rediscovered my interest in jazz and I had in fact been learning to play the drums since my return from Clacton, and when a group of my long-standing friends decided to form a band I was naturally keen to be included in this new venture. At this point I had to make a choice between getting fit enough to return to boxing, which meant getting out of bed at dawn and running for miles over Hampstead Heath in all weathers so that I could be fit enough to be punched at regular intervals, or spending late nights with the band playing and drinking and chatting up women. Boxing suddenly lost its appeal.

I quickly realised that I was the worst drummer on the planet; I just about managed to keep time. One of the first records I had bought however was Flamingo by Earl Bostick and he turned me on to the saxophone. Bostick played alto sax and I had also been listening to the great British tenor saxophone player Tubby Hays and it was listening to him that influenced me to switch to the tenor saxophone. My primary musical influences were the big bands that were very popular at the time. I was a competent saxophone player but my real interest was in becoming a musical arranger for big bands and I enrolled as a part time student at Trinity College where I studied theory and composition.

The role of the arranger is two-fold. The primary purpose is to take a written composition and transpose it so as to allow an orchestra to play it. Not all orchestras or bands are comprised of the same level of brass, woodwind, strings and rhythm sections of course, therefore band parts need to be written to suit. Secondly, the arranger must ensure that the finished work represents a musical style or overall sound that the orchestra leader wishes to portray as being individual to their particular orchestra. I particularly enjoyed arranging forties songs into a jazz style that suited our small six-piece band. The permanent members comprised myself (tenor saxophone), Don Forsythe (alto saxophone), Jim Fagan (trumpet), Frank Aquilina (trombone) and Harry Morris (drums); bass and piano would be taken up by whoever was available at any time.

My musical career was cut short however when all the band members, including myself, were called up for military service. I enjoyed my time in the army and it was in the service that I discovered that my previous boxing experience could prove useful. As a member of the boxing team I could swan about Aldershot in a tracksuit and when officers asked what I was doing out of uniform the answer was always, '*training for the boxing team sir*'. No officer ever questioned the fact that boxing team training appeared to be a full time occupation.

The military also proved to be my first experience of what was laughingly termed anti-terrorist training. This happened when I broke the military golden rule that says that you should never volunteer for anything. The fifties was a period when the IRA obtained most of their weapons by stealing them from military armories. The organisation had not yet developed the fund-raising skills in America that would enable them to purchase modern weapons.

Having been selected to join a team for the very important task of safeguarding the regimental armoury I expected to be issued with a weapon, but to my astonishment the team was issued with white pickaxe handles. How these items were supposed to deter armed terrorists was never explained. When we asked why the pickaxe handles were painted white, it was explained to us that this was done so that an officer making a snap check on us during the night could easily find us! The fact that it also identified us to the IRA in the dark was dismissed as being irrelevant.

An assumption by our officers that the IRA was frightened stiff of white pickaxe handles was eventually acknowledged to be fundamentally flawed however and a decision was subsequently made to issue us with weapons. Initially we were told that we were to be issued with the Lee Enfield 303 rifle that had been the main weapon of the British infantry throughout World War II, but at the last moment however this decision was changed. We were actually issued with Sten-guns, another World War II weapon capable of firing single shots or automatic bursts. We now felt far more confident to take on all-comers and so armed we moved to the ammunition store to collect our magazine rounds. We were somewhat surprised however to be told at this point that no ammunition was to be issued. This decision was taken apparently on the grounds that soldiers armed with automatic weapons loaded with live rounds might be dangerous! It appears that health and safety officials were alive and well as early as 1955.

With our safely unloaded weapons we continued to be a menacing deterrent to would be attackers for six months at various camps where an attack was considered possible. I would like to claim that our efforts prevented a terrorist attack but in reality the IRA had now discovered that they could easily purchase much better weaponry elsewhere and they now had the funds to do so. On a serious note however, I did learn much from the military. I attended numerous lectures on terrorism and terror groups. The knowledge that I picked up from this training would subsequently prove to be excellent grounding for a close protection role in civilian life. I did in fact return to the military some years later on a part time basis and I was astonished at the improvement in training and I was fortunate enough to take advantage of that training for free. This improved training included: risk and threat analysis and assessment, terrorist ideology and methodology, preparation and planning, fitness and first aid. Training required us to study the methods used by a wide range of terrorist groups following which we were allocated a particular organisation that we had to undertake in-depth research into. My particular task was to research the activities of the German Baader Meinhof group, named after Andreas Baader and Ulrike Meinhof, and deliver a lecture to the class on the 'Role of Women in Terrorism'. I kept my lecture notes and some years later I was invited to deliver the same lecture to a powerful women's group at the Cafe Royal in Piccadilly.

When I joined the army, initially dance halls, or ballrooms as some were called, where big bands played were enjoying tremendous popularity in spite of the fact that some ballrooms had a reputation for violence on a Friday night. While I had been busy protecting the nation's assets with an unloaded Sten gun however, new music cultures had emerged. I was aware

I was in training when this picture was taken. As the only sober one, I had to serve the drinks!

of the emergence of a form of musical culture that people called 'skiffle'. It appeared that skiffle could be performed by anyone with a cheap acoustic guitar and knowledge of three chords. The bass was usually a home made instrument made up of an upside down tea chest with a broom handle attached. String was then attached tightly from the top of the broom handle to the inside top of the tea chest. When the string was plucked the tea chest acted as a simple amplifier. To a person like me, who had aspired to become a musical arranger, this sub culture of folk music was little more

Defending the nation: Pat Beacon (A coy), Chip Warren (seated HQ coy), Geordie (above Chip B coy), myself (HQ coy), and Ray Donn (B coy) at Fulwood barracks, 1956.

than childish fun. When I came out of the army however I discovered that skiffle had become more professional thanks to jazz musician Lonnie Donegan who had a massive hit with the song, Rock Island Line, which was a hybrid of blues and folk music.

Perhaps more importantly I had missed the emergence of Rock 'n' Roll. By the time I had become a civilian Elvis Presley had changed the direction of Rock 'n' Roll. Britain had also produced its own first rock star in Tommy Steel who had young women screaming at shows all over the country after releasing his hit record 'Rock With the Caveman'. During the early sixties new British artistes such as Cliff Richard still copied Elvis but rock 'n' roll was changing direction again due to the influence of American acts such as Buddy Holly who is acknowledged by Paul McCartney to have been a major influence of the Beatles. This new music sub-culture would subsequently emerge in the UK to be popularly known as 'Beat Music' and it would prove to be source of income for me. Unfortunately it was also the cause of my giving up my aim to be a musical arranger as there was very little work for big bands – everyone wanted beat groups.

'The Bear' (left) supervising a river crossing during a military training exercise. I was the safety officer which meant that I had to suffer in a warm Land Rover with only a flask of coffee, while they enjoyed the cold.

During this musical evolutionary period I was making a living working on the close protection circuit, mainly with Arab clients. When work was not available I took on door work. Bouncers, or Door Supervisors as they prefer to be known today, do not receive a good press and the public tend to regard them as hooligans always looking to enjoy a fight. While some doormen have undoubtedly fitted this image, the great majority of those who I have worked with were just regular guys trying to earn a living. The job is extremely difficult as being polite to drunks with alcohol fuelled courage that leads them to think that they have absolute right to insult you, or worse still attempt to stab a glass in your face, is a job that not many people wish to take on.

During the period I worked on doors the police were reluctant to get involved with disorder at entertainment venues, they preferred to let the door staff sort it out. The Royal Ballroom, Tottenham, where I worked for a while was directly opposite Tottenham Police Station, but to the best of my knowledge they never once responded to the fights that regularly took place on a Friday night. The risk of injury to door staff from these situations is obvious; a friend of mine once told me that he had ended up in casualty every New Year's Eve for five years. He chose to share this information with me during a casual conversation when I had agreed to help him on the door of the Thatched Barn Disco in Borehamwood,

The band: Frank, Harry, Jim, me and Don.

Hertfordshire (now a hotel) one New Year's Eve. Fortunately nobody went to casualty that night. Some years later I attended the funeral of Dave Anderson, a promising young boxer who was murdered while working on the door of a club in North London. My understanding is that Dave simply went to question a young man who he thought might be dealing drugs. As he approached him the guy pulled a knife and fatally stabbed Dave and ran off. Sadly this is the sort of risk that door supervisors are regularly exposed to now.

When I started work at the Tottenham Royal venue management had obviously recognised a need to cater for rock 'n' roll or jive dancing as it was often called. A compromise was therefore in place whereby at the beginning of the evening a resident band would play 45 minutes of dance music, and at the Royal this was the Johnny Howard band. On completion of their set, the stage would revolve to reveal a beat group that would play for jivers. This cycle would continue until the resident band ended the evening with the last waltz, which gave young men their final opportunity to offer to escort a young lady home.

At the time I tended to regard this management policy of compromise to be very confusing. It appeared to me that we were attempting to cater to two opposing cultures and this inevitably led to confrontation. At a given signal one group of dancers would suddenly disappear from the dance floor and immediately the atmosphere would change as the floor was then taken over by a counter culture group. Forty-five minutes later the situation would all change again. Invariably the two groups would meet head on at some change-over point with the rockers the more volatile and at this point we had to get in quick to separate them.

Due to problems experienced with Teddy Boys at the Royal Ballroom prior to my employment, the management had a policy of banning them from the venue. Apparently they had been particularly violent and gangs were known to have used open razors and bicycle chains to inflict severe injury to their victims. A policy of banning them was very difficult to enforce however due to the fact that there were varying definitions of a Teddy Boy. It was not unknown to ban a person because he was wearing a particular type of tie, only for him to be allowed in ten minutes later by a different doorman who saw no problem with his dress. Fortunately this state of confusion was eased somewhat as Teddy Boy culture slowly subsided to become a minority cult that was happy to restrict their activities to specialised clubs that catered for their fifties style of rock 'n' roll.

I obviously needed to keep up my personal fitness during this period and a way of doing so and earning money was to act as a sparring partner for professional boxers. Professional fighters like Billy Walker needed heavyweight sparring partners to prepare for an upcoming fight. Normally I was paid £3 for every round and on average I sparred for three rounds in a gym session which was good money in those days. For those unfamiliar with boxing terminology, sparring requires you to assist the fighter by boxing with him so that they can practice their moves and tactics. I should add that the sparring partner is not supposed to inflict damage on the professional, as a serious cut, for example, could force him to cancel his next fight. A sparing partner would normally be picked because he is of the same height and weight as the fighter's next opponent. Occasionally however a lighter more agile sparing partner might be employed in order for the fighter to work on his speed and timing.

I usually trained at a gym run by the Boxing Board of Control, at Haverstock Hill, in north London. During one training session I meet up with Des Cox who I had been to school with. Des had turned professional and he had been sparring with the British heavyweight champion Henry Cooper. Henry had cracked Des's ribs practicing his famous left hook so consequently he was not able to spar which left Henry one sparring partner short. I was asked if I wanted to spar with Henry Cooper and not wishing to turn down £9 cash I accepted.

On the day, I arrived at the gym to find photographers present and it was explained to me that this sparing session was for the purpose of taking photographs for a school book on boxing Henry had agreed to publish. I had no objection but I was surprised to find that once in the ring all that was required was for Henry to pose his punches so that the photographer could snap them. It turned out to be the easiest sparring session I ever did and if I am economical with the truth when I tell the story I can claim that I once spared with Henry Cooper for three rounds and he never hit me once! Henry's manager, Jim Wicks, popularly known as the 'Bishop', did however try to avoid paying me. He offered me a free signed copy of the book when it was published, in lieu of my £9 fee. I told him that £9 had been agreed and that is what I wanted and he paid up. When I later told Des Cox the story he was not amused, as he had been paid the same fee for receiving two cracked ribs! Unfortunately the photographer got all the shots needed in that one session so there were no more punch-easy sparring sessions with Henry.

It is quite common for people in the boxing or wrestling game to get involved in film work and I also obtained some. I took part in episodes of three television programmes and one film and one television commercial. Film work paid well but I made the mistake of not applying for an Equity card. One day I was approached on a film set by a person who turned out to be the Equity representative who asked to see my card. Not having one I was asked to leave the set and I was turned down when I applied for a card on the grounds that I was not a trained actor.

Not deterred by the end of my somewhat brief acting career I carried on working at various pubs, clubs and dance halls around London. Working at these venues I was able to meet several entertainment people who in turn offered casual personal protection work with their clients. One of these contacts was Peter Walsh, the owner of Starlite Artistes, an agency that managed or represented many well-known acts of the period such as the Tremeloes, Marmalade and Billy Ocean. In association with Manchester promoter Danny Betesh, Peter Walsh promoted what I understand was the first theatre tour by The Beatles and I was employed to help out on a casual basis for the south of England dates. It was on the Beatles tour that I met Mal Evans who was responsible for the Beatles security. Mal had previously worked as a club doorman in Liverpool where he had met the group and I got on well with him. Sadly, however, Mal was killed in a shooting incident while on a trip to America.

Beatles' concerts were surprisingly free of crowd safety problems; the audience appeared to be content to stay in their seat space and scream throughout the performance. Theatre staff also appeared to have little problem keeping the audience in their seat space therefore private security companies were not involved in the early shows I worked on. Outside the theatre it was a different matter of course; the police were called in regularly to control huge crowds that gathered in the streets and at airports to catch a glimpse of their idols. At the shows crowd hysteria was regarded as being simply adolescents letting off steam, and while this behaviour was confined to controlled theatre environments there was no great cause for concern. My role therefore was confined to backstage security and getting the artistes in and out of the theatre. At the end of the show I would also collect the mass of toys, sweets and cards that had been thrown onto the stage and deliver it by the sack-full to the office. Not the most challenging of roles but it was better than fighting with drunks on a Friday night, and the pay was better.

I cannot claim to have known the Beatles intimately as my role was very much that of security backup. On one occasion however Paul McCartney arrived at Abbey Road Studios where he asked me to park his Roles Royce convertible. I took the keys and was just about to drive the car to a parking spot when he shouted, *"Stop"*. I immediately braked and Paul asked: *"You do work for me don't you?"* When I told him I did he said, *"Thank Christ for that – I thought I'd just given away a new roller"*.

My only claim to fame with regard to the Beatles therefore is that I once parked Paul McCartney's car! Some years later I was in charge of backstage security for a concert by Wings at Wembley Arena when Paul arrived with his wife Linda. My car parking ability had obviously impressed him because he came over to say hello and he told Linda that I had once worked for the Beatles!

Working on Rolling Stones concerts in the sixties I experienced many more crowd control problems than I did on Beatles' shows. The Rolling Stones began their career as a blues band circa 1962 but by 1963 the band had broadened their style to indicate a more Rhythm and Blues influence. The Stones were marketed as the antithesis of the Beatles acceptable image.

Originally the Stones appealed to an audience of mainly young women in much the same way as the Beatles but this quickly changed to a situation where the group appealed to a far greater proportion of young men. Working with the Stones at venues with low, easily accessible stages as I did during 1964 I found it to be a nightmare in terms of combating stage invasions from over-excited fans both male and female. Inevitably the reputation for disorder at Rolling Stones concerts affected the number of venues willing to accept their concerts. The Stones 1965 European tour is regarded by many people in the industry to have been a turning point in concert crowd behaviour due to the fact that riots inside and outside the venues were reported in a number of trade publications. For example, the Hit Parader magazine asked:

"The girls who flip over the current breed of pop singers seem to be much wilder than those who swooned over Sinatra or even the ones who

ripped Elvis Presley's clothing to shredded souvenirs. If this is the way audiences are blowing their cool over the Rolling Stones in 1965, how will the next generation of fans react?"

(Hit Parader, November, 1965)

Unfortunately this question was proved to be well founded, but not in quite the way that perhaps the reporter had envisaged. Just three years later, on the 6th December 1969, 18-year-old Stones fan Hunter Meredith was stabbed and beaten to death by Hells Angels employed to control the crowd at an open air concert at Altermont USA

At the time of the incident the Angels claimed they acted to prevent an assassination attempt on Mick Jagger by Hunter. This defence claim was widely discounted however. It appeared that Hunter was carrying a firearm but eye witness accounts of the incident testified that he (Hunter) drew a gun only after he had been stabbed and at this point he was running away from the stage to escape his attackers. It was alleged that once a firearm had been produced the Angles then attacked Hunter a second time.

During the seventies, violence at rock concerts thankfully became far less of a problem. Rock concerts were promoted on a much bigger scale at outdoor venues therefore far more tickets were available for the fans. Crowd hysteria at pop concerts remained a major problem however as I found out when I joined Artiste Services where I worked with David Essex, ABBA, The Osmond Brothers, David Cassidy, David Soul and many others. The mere sight of these artistes was guaranteed to create crowd chaos both *inside* and *outside* theatres.

The seventies was therefore the point at which a new leisure security industry began to learn new lessons in subjects that included the effects of high crowd density, crowd psychology and how to control large-scale pedestrian movement on grass and the measurement of ingress and egress capacities. These lessons were not learned without pain and it would take many more years before qualifications were introduced for the person who we now call the crowd manager.

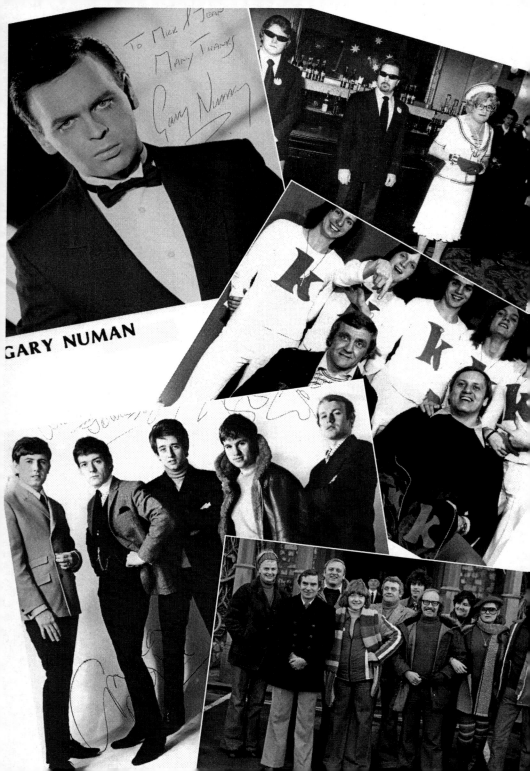

GARY NUMAN

To Mick & Jean
Many Thanks
Gary Numan

4 ARTISTES SECURITY SERVICES

From what we have seen in the pervious chapters it would appear that security at social events in the form of crowd control has been necessary since the ancient Greeks and Romans staged events. Historically however, crowd control was very much a casual service paid for by entrepreneurs. For an organised leisure security industry to exist it was first necessary to establish a formalised private security industry as a base from which this new security concept could evolve.

In his published research into the private security industry, Draper (1978) claims that the first private security company to be established in the UK was the Machinery and Transport Company formed in 1926 for the transportation of valuables. Draper goes on to claim that property protection was not considered until Night Watch Services, the forerunner of Securicor, was founded in 1935 to patrol houses in the Mayfair area of London. The development of the private security industry was naturally halted by the events of World War II during the period 1939-1945. The end of World War II saw a dramatic growth in the private security industry however when new companies mushroomed. With full time employment, private security companies established themselves as an industry but leisure security remained very much a casual occupation.

By the beginning of the 1950s the private security industry was broadly divided into three categories or functions. On one level there were registered companies that wished to provide an alternative service to the police. This would include guarding premises and valuables and such functions as retail security (store detectives). On another level a 'bouncer' culture was firmly established in flourishing clubs and dance halls to deal with troublemakers. This bouncer culture consisted of part-time casual workers normally recruited from the ranks of ex-boxers, wrestlers or local men with a tough reputation. Thirdly there was a long established practice whereby staff were employed by theatres, concert halls and sports grounds as stewards or ushers, a role that basically meant taking tickets and showing people to their seats. These three levels still exist today. What did not exist in the fifties was a professional leisure security industry that catered for specific crowd safety needs of mass crowd events and

Artiste Services team: Don, Wally, Danny, Roger, Pete, Mick.

the increasing demand for celebrity protection. As stated in the previous chapter, it was the impact of rock 'n' roll in the fifties that really created a social environment whereby a professional leisure security company could flourish.

In the UK the first company to be formed specifically to service the leisure industry was possibly Artistes Services, later to become Artistes Security Services. It is for that reason that the whole of this chapter is given over to a review of that company in acknowledgement of the important role that it played in establishing a whole new security concept. The model provided at the end of this chapter illustrates the lineage of the current leisure security companies and industry professionals that can be traced back to this one company.

At the height of its success Artistes Services (Artistes Security Services) was managed by a partnership of Don Murfet and Gerry Slater. In 1957 the internationally famous bandleader Vic Lewis employed Don Murfet as his band bus driver and road manager. In 1960 Vic Lewis started an artiste employment agency and Don was offered his first job as a Tour Manager with the American group the Platters who began that year with their first date at the Astoria Theatre Finsbury Park in North London.

In his autobiography, *Leave To Me*, published just before his untimely death from cancer, Don Murfet (2004) explains how he learned about show business by working with American stars of the day such as Tommy Roe and Johnnie Ray. He actually worked on the Johnnie Ray UK tour mentioned in the previous chapter. The Lewis agency would subsequently prove to be important in the evolution process of the leisure security industry due to the influential people who worked there. Don explains in his book that others involved in the agency based at 35 Curzon Street at that time included Don Arden, Vic Lewis, Micky Most, Barry Clayman, Don Black and Barry Dickens. All worked as agents, bookers or managers of acts. Any student of the entertainment industry will know that this list reads like a who's who of the music business. If these names were not enough, Peter Grant, later to become the legendary manager of Led Zeppelin, would join the agency working for Don Arden as a road manager for his acts.

Don Murfet decided to leave the agency in 1965 to set up Artistes Car Services. He felt it to be the right time to branch out and the aim of this new venture was to provide a luxury transport service with security and discretion for people in the entertainment industry. Naturally Don called on his friends at the booking agency to provide a client base. A measure of the importance of his contacts at the booking agency and the high regard that those there held for Don is the fact that just *some* of the early clients of the new company were the Beatles, Donavan and Led Zeppelin. A pretty spectacular start to a new company by anyone's standards.

Gerry Slater trained initially as a hairdresser and at the time Don set up his new venture Gerry owned and operated a hairdressing salon in Kentish Town, North London. It just so happened that June Murfet, Don's wife, was one of his clients and it was through June that Gerry became aware of Don's new business venture. Apart from a successful hairdressing business Gerry also had an interest in record retail outlets. In an interview for this book, Gerry recalls that the two men actually met for the first time when Don took the singer Tony Bennett to his record shop in East London as part of a record promotion campaign. During the visit Don mentioned that he was having a problem handling the level of work that he had and at this point a partnership was formed. Although the two men may not have realised it at that time, they were about to lay the foundation stone for what was to become a formalised leisure security industry that would set standards that many others (including myself) would follow some years later.

On tour with Led Zepplin. Alan Chandler can just be seen bottom right. Photo courtesy Ross Halfin

Artistes Car Services was based on the first floor above a greengrocer's shop rented from a member of June Murfet's family at Inverness Street, Camden Town. Overseeing office management and keeping everyone in order in what must have been a chaotic situation at times was Lyn Hutton. When celebrity protection began to exceed the demand for transport the partners sold their car company to Capitol Cars. They then channelled their efforts into what was now Artistes Services, later changed to

Lyn Hutton and Don Murfet.

Artistes Security Services. At this point the original drivers found themselves employed as security men; they no longer drove the car, they sat in the front passenger seat as client protectors. Lyn Hutton left the company when she married and moved to Australia. She returned seven years later however to once again take over office management at Artiste Security Services when Annette Kay (now Annette Robinson) left the company. Annette went on to establish herself as a successful event producer.

The immediate success of Artistes Services

meant that they quickly needed more staff and they brought in streetwise people who would subsequently become well known due to their constant media exposure and, it must be said, a clever marketing strategy by the partners. The names and photographs of these individuals regularly appeared in the press in stories of their exploits in protecting the most famous entertainment people of the day. The names of these people must be acknowledged here because they undoubtedly were the foundation stone of celebrity protection in the UK. Foremost among these people were Patsy Collins, Paddy and Jim Callaghan, Wally Gore, Fred (Fat Fred) Basset, Danny Fielding and Billy Francis. Each of these individuals was unique in so much as none of them had been formally trained for VIP protection. This fact was certainly not a drawback because they all had an understanding of the rock 'n' roll phenomena therefore they were all in tune with their clients needs and this made them very popular. What they did not know they quickly learned by experience. The role of celebrity protection and how that role has changed over the years is the subject of a later chapter.

The reputation of Artistes Services was undoubtedly founded on its ability to provide celebrity protection with discretion, which had been the aim of the company from day one. Unknown to Don and Gerry in the early days however the company would go on to achieve even greater recognition due to something that happened 3,000 miles away one year before Don Murfet took a decision to set up his celebrity car service.

In 1964 the commercial success of the Beatles had proved to be such that the final concert of their American tour was moved from an indoor arena to the Kansas City baseball stadium in order to accommodate the demand for tickets. This simple change of plan subsequently changed the scale of concert promotion forever. The following year the Beatles returned to America, and this time massive venues were scheduled into the tour, including the prestigious Shea Stadium, New York. Attendance figures for the Shea Stadium concert are estimated to have been 55,000 people. This would have been considered to be a phenomenal amount of people in 1965 when concerts were normally held in venues with a maximum capacity of 10/12,000 people. Film of the event shows that the crowd was restricted to the grandstands; the public was not allowed onto the pitch area. This practice would be considered to be very restrictive by audience expectation today. In addition to stadium staff, New York City

Police officers were employed in a crowd control role inside and outside the stadium.

The highly successful Beatles stadium concerts were a milestone in concert promotion because they alerted UK concert promoters to the potential profit to be gained by increasing crowd capacity even further. There were basically three possible ways that a commercially viable capacity could be achieve: use the pitch area of a sports ground to accommodate people, present concerts over a two- or three-day period, or promote them at a green-field site. All three options presented a problem however. During the sixties stadium operators would not permit the use of the pitch area, fearing that the playing surface might be damaged. But excluding the public from the pitch area would make stadiums unpopular with performers who preferred the crowd to be near to the stage. Stadiums were also expensive to hire for the period of two- or three- concert days. Consequently, staging what were called 'pop festivals' at green-field sites was seen as the solution and they proved to be, and still are, very popular.

My first experience of a green-field site event was when I first worked for Artistes Services in 1969 at a free concert given by The Rolling Stones in Hyde Park. Artiste Services provided protection for the band in terms of getting them from a nearby hotel to a stage in the middle of a crowd of 500,000 people, securing the stage and getting the band away safely. At this event the Stones tried an interesting experiment in crowd control. They employed a Hells Angels chapter to be responsible for front of stage security and crowd safety but unfortunately the Angels had little interest in crowd safety and Artiste Services staff was called on repeatedly to solve crowd control problems. At the end of that same year, the Stones tried using the Angels again in America at a concert on the 6th December 1969 at Altamonte. Reference has been made previously to the fact that 18-year-old Stones fan Hunter Meredith was stabbed and beaten to death at that event. An urgent need for a structured system of crowd safety management and security at such events had been reinforced.

One year later a need for crowd safety planning was again indicated when I undertook my next job for Artistes Security Services, again as a casual member of staff at a concert on the Isle of Wight in August 1970. There had been two successful concerts previously on the island in 1968 and 1969 but the 1970 event proved to be so problematic that local legislation was passed to effectively ban future mass crowd concert events. My recollections of that concert are primarily that the stage roof caught fire and there was no effective fire response plan and literally thousands of people arrived at the site without tickets. Non ticket-holders set up camp on a hill overlooking the site and they caused so many problems pulling down the arena fence that promoter and compere Rickki Farr went on the stage and declared the event to be a free concert.

When people did buy entry tickets, the huge crowds that attended greenfield site concerts compensated for the expense of constructing a temporary arena but pop festivals were proving to be the cause of many complaints due to the inconvenience and nuisance to locals. Subsequently, stadium operators, possibly realising that they were missing a lucrative market, allowed their pitch areas to be used by the public. One of the earliest sports grounds in the UK to open up fully for a concert event was Charlton Athletic Football Club which allowed The Who to play there in 1974.

The Who concert at Charlton Athletic was my first job as a regular member of the Artistes Services team. Don Murfet put me in charge of back stage security. It was my first major concert event as a manager, my previous experience being VIP protection and door supervision. The Charlton concert was a great learning curve for me because the job was more than a straightforward security role. I had to deal with dozens of massive egos demonstrated by desperate people wishing to get back-stage simply to boast that they had been there.

At one point I happened to be standing near to the back-stage vehicle gate when a Daimler limousine suddenly appeared with the chauffeur wildly sounding the car horn. Thinking that this must be a person of great importance the security guys immediately opened the double gates. As the car got halfway in my security instincts kicked in and I noticed that there was no car pass on display. I immediately halted the vehicle and demanded to see passes and at this point the passengers gave me a volley of abuse. In between shouts of abuse they told me that they were important personal guests of the promoter Harvey Goldsmith. Furthermore if I did not get out of the way immediately I would never work in this business again. Fortunately I had been in conversation with Harvey Goldsmith just prior to this outburst and he witnessed the whole incident. I could tell by his smile that Harvey had obviously never set eyes on these people before so I threw them and their hired limousine out.

In the years that followed I was to hear the outraged "*don't you know who I am*" rant many times from minor celebrities trying to get back-stage.

My usual answer was *"no I don't know who you are and what's more I couldn't care less who you are"*. To the best of my knowledge I never turned away a genuine person. One of the first lessons that I planned into training courses years later was how to deal with people determined to get back-stage and I often used the incident at Charlton to illustrate the point that a limousine and a lot of noise is usually a cover for a bluff.

The Who at Charlton also sticks in my memory as the time of the 'Free George Davis campaign'. George Davis was an armed robber who had been wrongly convicted of robbing the Ilford branch of the London Electricity Board. Subsequently a campaign was mounted to free him from an imposed 20-year prison sentence. Efforts to gain his release included damaging the cricket pitch at Headingley prior to a test match and spraying *'George Davis is innocent'* graffiti on walls all over London. Roger Daltry supported the campaign by wearing a 'Free George Davis' tee shirt on stage at Charlton. Davis was subsequently released from prison. Unfortunately however he was arrested and convicted a couple of years later for another armed robbery!

Following the success of the Who concert other sports grounds quickly followed the lead set by Charlton. By allowing approximately 15,000 to 20,000 people onto the pitch at a sports ground it was then financially possible to lose the seats at one end of a stadium so as to construct a proscenium stage. Sports grounds therefore offered a dual concept of seating for those who wanted it and standing for the fans that didn't, a popular practice that continues to this day.

By the seventies mass crowd attendances at pop and rock concerts at both green-field sites and sports grounds were commonplace. They were also the catalyst for the expansion of Artistes Security Services to become the largest event crowd control company in Europe. By the end of the seventies the partnership of Don Murfet and Gerry Slater had established their reputation as arguably the most knowledgeable event crowd managers in what at that time was referred to as rock 'n' roll security. Their services were in demand by rock acts such as Led Zeppelin and pop idols such as David Cassidy and The Osmond Brothers.

Sadly, however, a David Cassidy concert at the White City stadium in 1974 proved to be memorable for the wrong reason. The concert was attended by an estimated 30,000 people, mostly young females. Artiste Services was responsible for Cassidy's personal security and crowd control as usual. I was a member of the protection team. Don Murfet was Head of Security, Billy Francis was the Team Leader and Gerry Slater was the Tour Manager.

The concert is remembered by many people as the event at which a 15-year-old young woman tragically died following a crowd related incident. A study of this tragic accident is considered today to be essential training for would be crowd safety managers. It is for this reason that the accident and its repercussions, in terms of guidance introduced to make events safer, is the subject of another chapter.

The Cassidy White City concert was the first event at which a casual worker by the name of Ben Hatherall worked. Although he may not have realised it at the time Ben would go on to become a major influence in the logistical planning for many mass crowd events managed by Artiste Security Services. He was a serving soldier stationed at Knightsbridge Barracks when he accepted what was one-day casual employment as a steward at a pop concert. At that time military personnel were allowed to work in their off duty time and Ben had been promised £5 payment in cash. He witnessed the tragic accident but he was unaware of the tragic consequences at the time.

Ben was quick to realise, however, that large-scale events needed large-scale organisation, expertise and discipline of a level the army excelled at. As a Warrant Officer (senior non-commissioned officer) Ben was ideally placed to recruit off duty military personnel, organise transport to and from the gig and most importantly, keep everyone fed and watered, and this is exactly what he went on to do at many events.

In 1976 Artistes Security Services were awarded a contract to provide crowd management and crowd control services for a concert by the Rolling Stones at Knebworth. Estimated attendance was 100,000 people and I was Head of Security and Crowd Safety. Ben provided approximately 700 mainly military casual staff to steward the event. What he also introduced, possibly for the first time at a rock concert, was a structured management team. This was also the event at which communications were given serious consideration when the company hired six radios. When consideration is given to the fact that a major event today might use over a hundred radios on site, six sets seems ludicrous. At the time, however it was considered an important step in management practice. It might be argued therefore that the Stones at Knebworth in 1976 was the time and place that the leisure security industry in the UK took its first steps toward understanding the principle of command and control.

It is important to remember that at that time the company was employed to respond to all matters of security and safety. The major concert events that took place at venues such as Blackbushe, Knebworth and Donington in the seventies were also very important because that they alerted a fledgling leisure security industry to other important issues that needed an organised response. The first of these issues was illicit trading in the form of unauthorised food and merchandise vendors, who saw these events as a licence to print money.

At a Bob Dylan concert at Blackbushe Airport in 1978 merchandise vending rights were managed by Paul Pike who charged a fee to would-be vendors and allocated positions for vending points on behalf of promoter Harvey Goldsmith. I was Head of Security and Crowd Safety and at one point in the afternoon I discovered that Charlie Kray, elder brother of the infamous Kray twins had arrived on site and was in the process of setting up an unauthorised stall selling tee shirts. On my arrival at the stall I also discovered that Charlie had brought with him about a dozen very heavy looking guys.

Just as Paul and I were considering our options, Ben Hatherall arrived with three minibus loads of security and it looked like this was going to turn into a very nasty situation. I decided to keep the teams on their buses while Paul first spoke to Charlie Kray to explain that there was a fee payable. To my great relief it turned out that Charlie had no objection at all to paying a fee for selling rights and the guys with him were there to protect his cash and stock. A fee of £100 was promptly paid and a peaceful day was had by all.

At the early Knebworth concerts unauthorised food and merchandise trading was a huge problem due largely to a family that operated from Kings Cross. This family ran teams of hot dog and ice cream vendors operating in the West End of London and they had a very heavy reputation. Concert promoter Freddy Banister was determined that they would not work on his events and precious security resources were constantly being diverted to chase these traders. Once again negotiation rather than confrontation solved the problem. An agreement was reached with Billy B... (one of the brothers) that when vendors were caught they pack up and move on peacefully. This had the effect of one steward being able to solve a problem rather that sending teams of security guys to confront the offender. The vendors constantly changed position of course but they were far less of a problem. As a result of my negotiations with the brothers, a somewhat bizarre situation developed. During periods of event build up and de-rig we were on friendly terms, often sharing a cup of tea and a sandwich, but on show day they became the opposition and we would continue our cat and mouse game.

Donington Monsters of Rock was different however, the traders who worked the event were from Nottingham and they were not interested in negotiation. They did pay a fee to trade but they constantly used every trick in the book to add unauthorised traders or flaunt health and safety regulations. On one occasion Ben Hatherall received heavy threats when he cautioned them about a failure to comply with safety standards. The situation was only resolved when the traders realised that Ben had about 600 people to back him up if it came to violence. Shortly after this the main trader was shot dead outside his house in Nottingham when he returned from an event late at night. It was speculated that rival traders, seeking to take over his business, shot him.

The safe collection and storage of cash was a major security problem during the ticket selling period and actual event in the seventies. In those days tickets were issued out to authorised ticket sellers around the country and the cash return had to be collected by the promoter at regular intervals. Andy Ayres, who was a Production Assistant for the Knebworth shows, recalls how he would drive around the ticket outlets collecting cash in carrier bags, which were deposited in the car boot after each collection. Fortunately, Andy was never robbed and that problem was solved largely to the popularity of credit card booking. The safe storage of cash on site at bars and other outlets was a major problem that required security. In case anyone is thinking of robbing a site today you should know that current practice is to employ cash in transit specialists who remove cash regularly in small amounts. Another idea gaining popularity is for the public to purchase plastic discs prior to the event, which can then be exchanged for goods or drinks during the show. Consequently there are very few cash transactions on site.

Campsites were another problem that site security teams had to contend with. Literally hundreds of people would arrive as early as the Monday for a Saturday show. This meant that the promoter was responsible for the provision of toilets, drinking water, firewood, fire control and welfare services. At the very early green-field site events there was little or no consideration given to the fact that people would camp. At first, efforts were made to prevent camping by closing off the site but all this did was move the problem further away and upset local farmers. Promoters and local authorities simply had to come to terms with campers as a fact of life.

Not all of my memories of early green-field site events are doom and gloom. My lasting memory of a Genesis concert at Knebworth in 1978 concerns a temporary building. Don Murfet was a great one for innovation and at the time of the Genesis show he informed us all that he had meet a guy who was going to supply us with a revolutionary new type of temporary structure to serve as our control room and office at Knebworth. This structure was igloo shaped and would sit on the top of a scaffold deck with a commanding view of the site.

Two days before the show a truck turned up with the necessary scaffolding equipment and a mass of white triangular plastic parts that we were told would be assembled into an office. The scaffold frame was assembled very quickly and Gerry Slater and I left the rigging crew to their job. As time went on however I began to notice that there was no work being done on the structure, furthermore the crew seemed to have disappeared. On the day before show day Gerry and I were now getting worried so we decided that we would build the thing, after all it cannot be that difficult as we had all the parts. Unfortunately it then began to rain heavily but undaunted we both carried on. Unfortunately the finished product looked as if a person under the influence of LSD had assembled it! Lyn Hutton arrived on site to find that she had to make an undignified climb up a ladder in the rain to reach the top, as our structure did not include stairs. When she reached the top she then found that she had to climb over a scaffold safety rail to get into the igloo office. To make matters worse it began to rain again and our handy work leaked like a sieve and there was no window. Typical Lyn, she took it all in her stride with only the occasional derogatory comment about our expertise in the building trade. Strangely, the igloo remained on its scaffold perch long after the show had finished. We would get regular calls from Knebworth estate asking when it would be gone but we were not able to contact the owner. Some weeks later I visited the site to find that it had simply disappeared. I use the word 'disappeared' deliberately because nobody on site had seen it dismantled and removed.

By 1979 our logistical planning had reached a level whereby the company was able to provide 800 staff, a control room with a functional radio network and an admin office to manage two weekend Led Zeppelin concerts at Knebworth. Each of these shows attracted an estimated attendance of 100,000 people. The band arrived by helicopter, which meant additional security and safety measures needed to be in place at the helipad.

At the first show however, the legendary Zeppelin guitarist Jimmy Page arrived in a separate helicopter after all the others members of the band and their entourage had arrived. Having landed, and finding himself alone at the helipad, Jimmy asked the security team the way to backstage. Not recognising him, the team offered to give him a lift in their van provided he didn't mind the fact that they needed to drive around the site dropping off relief security staff. Jimmy happily agreed and jumped into the back of a transit van with the security team and was driven off on a tour of the site. When the van eventually reached the backstage area the production team was stunned to see Jimmy Page climbing out of the back of a transit van. Everyone rushed to apologise for failing to send a limousine for him but he just laughed and said that he had actually enjoyed his trip and chat with the lads.

The Zeppelin Knebworth concerts were hard work and great experience, although for two of us they were also a painful memory. Just before the band was due to go on stage at the last show I made my usual routine check to ensure that the route from the dressing room to the stage and the stage itself was clear for the artiste. On checking the stage I noticed a fan had somehow managed to get onto the stage and was hiding in the truss stage right. This was not the biggest problem in the world and I simply signalled him to come out and leave. He seemed a bit nervous but nevertheless he came out. Just as he reached me he suddenly produced a short piece of scaffold and hit me across the left shoulder. Other members of the security team captured the guy and when asked why he had done it his excuse was that he thought that I might hit him so he got in first! I took no further action as the guy was obviously a devoted Zeppelin fan rather than a terrorist and I saw out the show with a very sore shoulder. At the end of the show the band piled into two jeeps and at a signal from their Tour Manager Richard Coles, they sped off, only to run over the foot of security team member John Ferguson. Later that night both John and I sat in the casualty department at the Lister Hospital comparing injuries. I have to say that his broken foot was far worse that my cracked shoulder bone, he was in plaster for weeks. In spite of our injuries we both took it to be just another rock 'n' roll working day.

As staff changes took place at Artiste Services new people moved in to take their place. Foremost among this new blood were Alan Chandler who had actually worked previously for the company, Ron Franklin and his two

Don Murfet looking suspiciously at my dodgy shirt.

Ben Hatheral Jerry Judge, Mick Upton and Alf Weaver at a Showsec anniversary party.

cousins Terry and John Franklin, Danny Francis (brother of Billy Francis), Dave Moulder, John Ferguson and Bob Maxey. Each of these individuals would go on to establish a solid reputation for expertise in the leisure security industry.

Ben Hatherall and the author at a regimental dinner.

As stated previously, Lyn Hutton had resumed work at the company and during my time with Artiste Security Services Lyn appeared to hold down three jobs: admin manager, personnel officer and finance/credit control manager. While we security staff would constantly bask in the glory of press articles that greatly inflated, and in some cases blatantly lied, about our ability, Lyn provided the driving force that went largely unrecognised. At this point the company had moved into club door supervision and clients included such prestigious venues as Legends, The Embassy, Peppermint Park and numerous other high profile venues in London. These venues were open most nights of the week and they paid good money, therefore they required suitable staff and strict credit control.

In addition to the club work the company took on a new contract when enterprising promoters from Southgate, North London, opened up Caister Holiday Camp during the winter period for theme weekends. This was a new concept that required a blend of discrete security and crowd safety management. The events were underpinned by concerts but they inevitably ended up as all night chalet parties which could get out of hand if not handled firmly. Ben Hatherall managed virtually all of these weekend events and true to form he again proved to be a master of logistical planning and event management.

This was also the period in which the company took on the in-house security and crowd control contract at the Rainbow Theatre, Finsbury Park, North London. I worked many times on this contract and once again it was Lyn who booked the large number of staff that were often required and managed credit control. In short, if a client did not pay their bill he wasn't unduly worried about the company sending the boys round but if Lyn called they always paid rather than risk a lecture from her.

My time at the Rainbow Theatre was during a period when punk rock was popular. Although punk fans received a bad press in my opinion, this was not entirely justified. Punks simply wanted to do what their parents before them had done, they simply wanted to dance. Unfortunately the Rainbow was a seated venue and the local authority insisted that the seats remain in place. Consequently we had regular re-runs of what cinemas had suffered during the introduction of rock 'n' roll. Once a band came onto the stage everyone would be on his or her feet and climbing over seats which promptly collapsed. The local licensing authority saw only one answer, more security, but this just brought about conflict between stewards and the audience. The simply answer was to remove the seats for punk concerts and the local authority finally allowed this to be done, just in time for the punk craze to finish!

I cannot let my time at the Rainbow go by without acknowledging the dedication of Alan Chandler who managed the auditorium floor. Alan never once let me down in all the often hairy shows that we did together. John Sibley also did sterling work, not only during the shows but often working throughout the night to repair or install seating ready for the next show. Mick Bowles managed the stage door effectively in spite of the verbal abuse he often received from disgruntled non-pass holders and Bob (The Emperor) Maxey could always be counted on when the going got tough.

Not all of the individuals mentioned in this chapter work in the leisure security industry now. Of the original drivers employed by the car company that went on to work for Artistes Services, Ray Washborn subsequently left to work as a PA for Peter Grant of Led Zeppelin management fame. Alf Weaver left to team up with Mike Conway to form M&A Security (Mike & Alf) and he later wrote a book about his experiences. When Jerry Judge took Mike Conway's place as a partner the company name M&A came to mean Music and Arts. Brendan Cahill emigrated to America where he worked for Columbia film studios; he sadly died in 2005. Patsy Collins was tragically killed in an incident in Indonesia on January 29th 1976. He fell down a hotel lift shaft. I never really knew Patsy, as I joined Artiste Services in 1973 and at that point he was constantly abroad on tour. I did meet him however and it is a measure of the man that reports of his death indicate that after falling down six floors he managed to climb out of the lift shaft to the hotel lobby in an attempt to get to hospital. He apparently then managed to reach the street where he climbed into a vehicle, which got him to hospital. Sadly he died of his injuries in the early hours of 30th January. The verdict was accidental death.

Of the other members of the Artistes Services team, Jim Callaghan left to work for the Rolling Stones and eventually set up Call-A-Hand Security, his brother Paddy subsequently joined him there. The company was then merged with ShowSec International but Jim and Paddy returned to working as independent tour security. Danny Fielding eventually left and spent time working with Tottenham Hotspur Football Club. Wally Gore moved to Call-A-Hand and then on to ShowSec. Wally has now retired except for the odd occasion when he gets called out of retirement by ShowSec. Fred Basset no longer works in the industry as far as I am aware. At the time of writing, Billy Francis is the Tour Manager for Sting. Of the later members to join the team, Alan Chandler now runs his own car service company. Ron Franklin ran a successful VIP car service for a while but is currently working for George Michael. Terry and John Franklin no longer work in leisure security. Bob Maxey worked for ShowSec for some years but now works independently. Dave Moulder married and settled in Spain where he now deals in antiques. John Ferguson also bought a home in Spain but was subsequently forced by ill health to remain in England. Lyn Hutton and Ben Hatherall settled down together; neither of them work in the leisure security industry now.

I left Artiste Services in 1982 to form ShowSec. In 1988 I purchased Artiste Security Services and the company ceased trading and Gerry Slater joined me at ShowSec as my partner where we successfully continued to provide large scale event crowd management and celebrity protection until we both retired and sold the company in 2000. Don Murfet sadly died as a result of Multiple Myeloma in March 2005.

During my 'apprenticeship' at Artistes Services I was privileged to learn a great deal, most notably the fact that there was a whole side of the security industry, known then as rock 'n' roll security, that I had previously known nothing about. Don Murfet and Gerry Slater were, in my opinion, the pioneers of implementing what we know to be crowd management, rather than simply carry on using crowd control strategies that had been in use since the days of the Roman Empire.

At this point it would seem appropriate to consider the terms 'crowd management' and 'crowd control' as both terms are used frequently

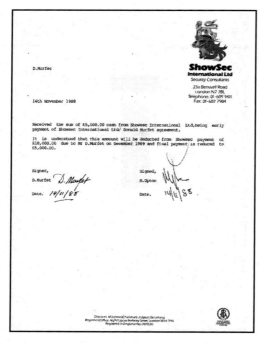

throughout this book. The highly respected American crowd safety planner John J. Fruin (1992) argued that, although the terms crowd management and crowd control are often used interchangeably, there are important differences. Fruin defined crowd management to be:

"*The systematic planning for, and supervision of the orderly movement and assembly of people. It involves the assessment of the people handling capabilities of a space prior to its use. It also includes the assessment of projected levels of occupancy, adequacy of means of ingress and egress, processing procedures such as ticket collection and expected types of activities and group behaviour*"

Fruin defines crowd control to be simply:

"*The restriction or limitation of group behaviour*".

The definitions provided by Fruin are accepted and endorsed by the membership of the United Kingdom Crowd Management Association (UKCMA) and the Centre for Crowd Management and Security Studies (BCUC) as appropriate in the their efforts to introduce training standards for leisure security staff.

The early recognition of these important differences was the bedrock of Artistes Security Services although they did not necessarily use these terms. It was nevertheless at Artistes Services that I first began to come to terms with issues such as crowd psychology and crowd dynamics and the need for training to implement command and control of a mass crowd event. On a broader perspective it was also a time when it was realised that an event required a team approach that included security for bars and the prevention of unauthorised trading, welfare services, campsite safety, car parking specialists and crowd safety specialists. Today it is standard practice to use specialist teams for these services not just one company.

The model shown illustrates the important influence that Artiste Services had in establishing a whole new security concept.

The model below illustrates the influence that Artistes Services had on a new leisure security industry.

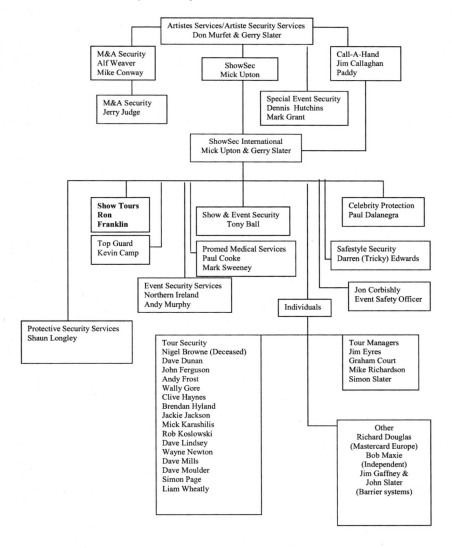

5 CREATING AN INDUSTRY

The previous chapter illustrated how what was once called rock 'n' roll security began. This chapter examines how an idea moved forward to create an industry with an annual turnover that can be estimated in millions of pounds and employs thousands of people. The growth of the leisure security industry since the seventies is undeniable. International companies now exist to provide services that include security, personal protection, crowd management and crowd control services. The client base for this industry is drawn from the world of film, television, music, sport, modelling, stage and that indefinable category of people that have become celebrities for no apparent reason other than appearing on a reality television show. This chapter looks at how a few of these companies followed in the wake of Artistes Services to create that industry.

It would not be possible to include all existing leisure security companies here; new companies start up and old ones merge or cease to trade on a seemingly regular basis. In this chapter I have chosen to review companies that, in my opinion, have demonstrated particular skill by the owner(s) in identifying areas of leisure activity that required security and crowd safety expertise. This does not imply that each of these companies is restricted to one particular type of event now, in a harsh commercial climate all companies undertake a broad range of leisure security activities in order to exist. Rather it is intended to illustrate the entrepreneurial flair of the individuals who created new markets rather than simply compete by offering lower charge rates to clients. The company profiles presented here are based on unstructured interviews with company operators and the information relating to a particular company has been provided and approved by each individual operator.

The companies and individuals that I have selected to review in this chapter are: Rock Steady, for creating arguably the first leisure security company in Scotland; ShowSec International for introducing training programmes; Goldrange for recognising a need for customer care at English football grounds; Show & Event Security for their crowd safety management expertise at street events; Special Event for their work at horse racing events; and Olympus Security for their work on reality TV shows.

The logic applied to this selection is that it demonstrates the broad range of leisure security services that are now offered by established companies.

Rock Steady

While Artiste Services was enjoying a well-deserved reputation for reliable crowd management, crowd control and celebrity protection in England in the seventies a young man by the name of Mark Hamilton was regularly attending events in Scotland. During his early observation of concert events Mark immediately spotted a fundamental flaw in the way that audiences were treated. In his words, *aggressive tactics were employed to control audiences who had, in his view as teenager, paid good money with the intention of enjoying themselves rather than wishing to cause a fight* (Hamilton 2006).

Mark Hamilton's career in leisure security began during the first half of the seventies when he took up casual employment as a member of an in-house concert steward team. His ability to organise and his attitude toward audience safety rather than simply enforcing crowd control strategies were quickly noticed and he was asked more and more to supervise or put together teams to manage events. Subsequently his approach to crowd safety management and event security was recognised by leading concert promoters and venue managers as being somewhat unique in Scotland and this encouraged him to start a company. He chose the name Rock Steady for his new company as it perfectly illustrated a service concept that was dependable and safe.

With the support of highly rated promoters such as Regular Music, Harvey Goldsmith, Marshall Arts, Kennedy Street, and venues that included the prestigious Edinburgh Playhouse, Mark nurtured and then developed Rock Steady into an organisation made up of very experienced and knowledgeable people. Many of these people are still with the company to this day. Particular mention must be made at this point of Fred Cucchi, who worked initially as a steward, left to form his own successful security company and subsequently returned to Rock Steady to take up a position as Operations Director. Others that have contributed greatly to the success of Rock Steady are Jim MacDonald and Peter Croy who are both long standing Senior Operations Managers.

Over the years I worked many times with Rock Steady and although we were at all other times competitors it is greatly to the credit of all members of the company that they always gave 110% dedication to the tasks allotted to them. There have been a number of times when I have been grateful to the Rock Steady team and one particular occasion always springs to mind when the company is mentioned. In 1988 I was employed as Head of Security and Crowd Management for a series of 15 major outdoor Michael Jackson concerts. One of my responsibilities was to employ local security companies where necessary. For a show at the Aintree racecourse, Liverpool, I was asked by the police to allocate work to local companies due to high unemployment in the city. Naturally I agreed. Subsequently a consortium of six security companies, approved by the local police, was awarded a contract to provide a total of 300 staff. I set a limit of 300 because I did not know the companies and therefore the remaining 400 staff required were contracted from companies I knew. My own company was only able to provide a limited number of staff due to prior commitment on other events. The companies contracted that I knew were Mark Hamilton (Rock Steady), John Jones (J J Security, Stafford) and Alan Willits (Concert Security, Birmingham).

Unfortunately on show day a couple of the local firms proved to be, shall we say, 'unreliable' to a level where I was forced to sack two companies halfway through the day. This amounted to leaving me approximately 100 staff short. However, pressure was off of the gates as the full capacity was now in the venue, which meant that I could afford to take a chance on a reduced staff level. The other teams all pulled together filling the gaps by cutting meal breaks short and we managed to make the show work.

A big problem was yet to come however. The two companies that I had sacked took exception to my decision and they threatened to put both Michael Jackson and me in hospital after the show. Sure enough, at the end of the show approximately 100 very angry ex-security men were gathered at the backstage gate. The police put in a strong presence which enabled us to get Michael Jackson away safely but unfortunately every police officer then left immediately after that leaving half a dozen ShowSec staff and approximately 50 of the Rock Steady crew to face the mob. After a quick backstage chat with my business partner Gerry Slater, event coordinator Tony Ball and Jim MacDonald we took the decision to 'front it out' as they say in the trade. So together we marched straight through the angry mob to the car park. Although there were was much abuse hurled at us the locals fortunately decided that they did not fancy taking on a team that were now getting very annoyed at what they regarded as a hindrance to their long journey home to Scotland after a hard day's work. And I was very glad to head south.

Mark Hamilton can be justly proud of the fact that he has achieved his aim of creating a company that consistently delivers a planned, organised and accountable crowd management system for the benefit of people attending a vast range of public gatherings from school fetes to world-class sports events and super scale concerts. Current information on Rock Steady Security can be found at www.rocksteady.co.uk.

ShowSec International

Given the fact that ShowSec International is a company that I started and was proud to act as Chairman of until my retirement in 2000, I naturally know a great deal about the company. I cannot claim to have had the same ambitions as Mark Hamilton, however, as the company started more by accident than design. I left my position as Head of Security at Artistes Services in 1981, my reason for leaving being the fact that I was not able to reach agreement with Don Murfet over terms for my new contract. There was no other reason for my leaving and Don and I remained friends up until his untimely death. At the time that I resigned from Artistes Services, Gerry Slater had already resigned his directorship and was focusing on artiste management and the provision of transport for artistes. My intention was simply to return to working independently on the close protection circuit.

In 1976 however I had began working for BBC TV while still with Artiste Services. Once I left the company I was contacted by producer John Laine who invited me to take over the security and crowd safety role for outside broadcast of the children's programme Swap Shop. At this point I was operating from home. My wife Jean handled telephone calls and kept the books with the support of Brenda Dunkly, a family friend who helped out with admin. When necessary I called in friends to help operationally.

Within a year I was working regularly, providing crowd control and celebrity protection services for BBC TV outside broadcast programmes, working on a casual basis on programmes that included: Going Live, Live and Kicking, sports programmes such as Super Stars and Super Teams, entertainment programmes such as Noel Edmonds' House Party and the comedy programme Only Fools and Horses.

The name ShowSec came about accidentally when John Laine advised me that the BBC would only accept a registered company for a contract. I am afraid that I lied when I told him that I was registered and when he asked the name of the company I quickly answered ShowSec. It was the only name I could think of on the spur of the moment. Things worked out fine however; I registered the company and spent the next nine years working on a part time basis for BBC TV outside broadcasts with the capable assistance of friends. Ron Vince undertook to help me on the early shows and later Martin Kerwin took over from Ron.

I enjoyed my time working with TV outside broadcast crews and I learned a lot in terms of how important crowd movement was, so as to clear people from camera shot, or alternatively to have them in the background for what the director called 'interesting shots'. On one occasion I was working with a TV crew at Nottingham Castle and predictably we had a Robin Hood character on the programme who was due to demonstrate his skill with a bow and arrow. The archer advised me on the safe distance that he required the watching crowd to be away from the target and I moved the crowd accordingly. Just before he was about to shoot at the target, however, I had second thoughts and I decided, for some unknown reason, to move the crowd further to one side. The archer shot his arrow on cue and somehow managed to miss the target completely. The arrow landed right where the crowd had been standing before my second move. Had I not moved the crowd it's possible that people watching at home would have seen a person shot by an archer on a live children's television programme! The archer was naturally very shaken and I kept the arrow as a souvenir.

Some months after I had left Artistes Services I had also been contacted by Paul Crockford who was then a partner in the Outlaw Agency, a young company that promoted shows and represented artistes. Paul asked me to oversee security at their shows. The Outlaw Agency was keen to get established in the tour market and to that end they put together a tour for the punk band Sham 69. Unfortunately the band had a poor reputation on the tour circuit, due mainly to problems caused by a hard core of their fans who were actually friends of the band. This group traded on their friendship, they never bought a ticket and they constantly abused the promoter's hospitality. The band also had a reputation for being extremely right wing, which I subsequently discovered, was unjustified. Paul Crockford asked me to take on the role of tour security and together with my good friend Dave Moulder we set off around the UK with the band.

Dave Moulder and I played the bad guys in terms of making these so-called friends pay for tickets and we barred them from backstage. The band played their good guy role by protesting to their friends that Dave and I were employed by their management and could not be dismissed. After a short period things settled down and the tour proved to be successful. I then found myself being introduced by Paul King, a partner in the Outlaw Agency, to Tony Elliot, owner of Time Out magazine as a person capable of handling difficult situations. It appeared that Elliot was having a few problems with a strike by staff at Time Out. The strikers had occupied his offices in Covent Garden and he was worried that they might decide to damage very expensive computer equipment. I was asked if I could get into the top floor offices undetected by the strikers, fix a security lock on the computer room door and then provide security on the room until the strike was settled.

After terms were agreed I chose Ron Franklin and his cousins Terry and John to help in the operation. Getting into the building at 03:00hrs was not difficult, all the strikers were asleep and we soon had a security lock fixed on the door. When the strikers woke up they were amazed to find a security team sitting outside the computer room drinking flasks of coffee. In fairness it must be said that nobody had made any attempt to damage the computers and, apart from a hard core group of three or four people, most strikers were pleasant toward us. Consequently I was able to reduce security cover to two men 24/7. A rather bizarre situation then developed over the next few days. The majority of the strikers were either married or simply fed up with having to sleep on an office floor and more and more of them started to go home at night. It reached a point where I contacted the owner to tell him that the office was unoccupied during the night and he could take it over any time he wished. He felt however that such a move would damage the credibility of Time Out and he preferred to let the strike run its course. We ended up in a situation where the strikers would say goodnight to us and all go home. In the morning they would come in and make us fresh coffee. Eventually the strike ended amicably and all but the ringleaders went back to work. I am pleased to say that it was possibly the most civilised industrial dispute ever.

As I moved into the early eighties things were going well. I undertook celebrity protection assignments with artistes who included Gary Numan, Elton John, Barry Manilow and rock band Whitesnake. It was also the time that I managed my first Donington Monsters of Rock concert as ShowSec. By the middle of the decade I had convinced Gerry Slater to join me in a partnership at what we re-branded as ShowSec International Ltd. In addition Ron Franklin became Operations Manager and shortly after

My daughter Jayne was Finance Director at ShowSec International until the company was sold.

that my daughter Jayne, who had trained in accountancy, joined the company as the Finance Director. Gerry Slater's youngest son Simon subsequently joined the firm and to his credit he started at the bottom and worked his way up to a management position. Simon is now an established independent tour manager and Ron Franklin went on to run his own specialist transport company. At that time we decided on a name change. A company was not allowed to use words like 'international' or 'worldwide' unless it could provide evidence that it was true statement of fact. As we were now sending tour security personnel abroad on a regular basis we had no difficulty in obtaining permission to use 'International' in the company title.

The eighties proved to be both challenging and rewarding. In the summer of 1985 we were contracted by the Harvey Goldsmith organisation to undertake the mammoth task of overseeing security at Live Aid. Originally we were told that the show would be staged at the Milton Keynes Bowl. This meant that ShowSec would have to provide a minimum of 600 staff and be responsible for crowd management planning. A few weeks before the intended date, however, I was contacted by the production manager Andrew Zweck who informed me that the show would now take place at Wembley Stadium. This change of venue was fine with me because it meant that we now only had to provide 200 staff. Wembley would take care of all crowd movement issues. The bad news was that Andrew then asked if we would do the show for free! It is greatly to their credit that all our staff agreed and every single one of them gave 100% commitment in spite of that fact that they were not being paid. I was disappointed therefore that not one of the subsequent articles, books, radio and TV programmes devoted to Live Aid thought it important to mention the fact that over 100 members of our staff had given their services freely.

ShowSec took on a series of major events during the eighties and nineties that would establish the company as a leading player in the provision of event crowd management, crowd control and celebrity protection. Tony Ball joined the company following completion of military service and initially he acted as my assistant. He learned quickly and was eventually appointed Operations Director. Contracts undertaken during this period included Bruce Springsteen's UK dates (1985), Live Aid (1985), Queen at Knebworth (1986), Wham The Final (1986), U2 (1987) dates and 15 major concerts for Michael Jackson (1987). During the nineties the company managed major events such as the two Oasis shows at Knebworth (1996) performed in front of 250,000 people who were reported in the musical trade press as a defining moment in Britpop. During this period of company development there were many people that contributed toward our success. In terms of event management however Steve Heynes provided great support. Steve was a sergeant in the army at the time and he came on board to take charge of our event control rooms where he installed some much-needed military style discipline into our control room management systems.

In November 1988 I purchased Artistes Services from Don Murfet for the sum of £10,000. Don Murfet had become manager for Adam Ant and he naturally became far more interested in artiste management. As a result of the purchase Bob Maxie joined ShowSec from Artistes and he acted as the London Manager until he left to go freelance at the end of the nineties.

The summer of 1988 also found ShowSec once again back at the Donington Monsters of Rock. Previous Monsters events had been challenging but very enjoyable. The 1988 event, however, will be sadly remembered primarily for the fact that two young men died tragically in a crowd crush accident at the front of the stage. This terrible tragedy was the catalyst for new guidance for concert events and the accident is covered in the form of a case study in a later chapter. The accident was also the event that convinced me that the industry needed to formalise training for crowd safety. Gerry Slater and I set up the ShowSec Training Wing where we researched, designed and delivered training programmes. Assisting

Jon (JC) Corbishly.

me in my efforts to introduce training was Jon (JC) Corbishly who would go on to graduate in 2005 as one of only two Safety Officers in the UK to hold a Foundation Degree in Crowd Safety Management. Subsequently we purchased a large old house in the village of Kilnsey, North Yorkshire, where we set up a residential training school. My daughter Jayne and her partner Mick Sheehan, who moved up from London, ran the school.

The ShowSec Training Centre, as we called it, proved to be very popular with foreign companies interested in training. People that attended the school came from South America, the USA and Holland and of course the various regions that we had by now established ShowSec offices. Many of the individuals that are well-established names in leisure security today attended training at Kilnsey. Our British competitors were understandably less interested. They felt that by sending their staff to us for training it implied that we were better than them. Consequently they preferred to introduce their own training programmes. Nevertheless ShowSec International did go on to achieve five awards for standards of service to the industry. The ShowSec training wing continues to prosper today under the guidance of Roy Wise, a graduate of the BCUC Crowd Safety Management FD course.

Sergent Malcolm Ding (now Inspector) and Sgt Ian Ellison (Essex Police) who Jon Corbishly and I worked with to produce what I understand to have been the first crowd safety management course for police officers. Previous police training focused on crowd control.

The eighties and the nineties were exciting times for ShowSec. We sent teams abroad to manage events in Germany, Portugal, Russia, Brazil, and Oman. In addition we had individuals constantly providing personal security for artistes touring the world. It was not all fun and glamour however. We were called on a number of times to provide crowd control and security for several funerals where it was anticipated that a large crowd would turn up. The most notable funeral that ShowSec worked on was that of Diana Princess of Wales in 1997.

In the early stage of discussion we were asked just to provide stewards for crowd control as the funeral procession passed through South Carriage Drive, Hyde Park. We were informed that the police might become over stretched due to the fact that at least one million people were likely to line the four-mile route from Kensington Palace to Westminster Abbey. It became obvious during subsequent conversations, however, that the government were having serious problems recruiting and coordinating the estimated 800 stewards necessary to man the route and we were asked to take on this role and we accepted. Steward teams were then brought in from as far away as Newcastle and agreement reached with senior officers at Scotland Yard on where they should be deployed. Unfortunately however, communications with the Metropolitan Police on the day were not what we expected. For example, we deployed 200 stewards to the Mall, to be positioned by a local police commander as agreed. Unfortunately this commander absolutely refused to allow stewards to work on a public street and no amount of radio messages back and forth to Scotland Yard could resolve the issue. Consequently 200 stewards were paid to sit in the park and do nothing. The story has a sequel however. The same commander approached me after the funeral was over to ask if we would supply stewards to the same area of the Mall throughout the night, as his officers were required to rest! We did provide staff to man the road-blocks in place around the Mall and Buckingham Palace until police officers arrived at 0600hrs to take over the positions.

By the year 2000 Gerry and I finally decide it was time to sell up and retire. We subsequently accepted an offer from Bert van Horch, a Dutch guy who at that time was the Chairman of the Security Company Holland and the two companies now work closely together. Bert has since sold his interest in ShowSec. The company is owned today by One Nation and is managed by Mark Harding, who has been with the company since the eighties and another graduate of the FD course. Regional Managers Simon Battersby and Mark Logan also graduated from the course. Under Mark Harding's guidance the company has moved more toward venue contracts, while the company still undertakes casual major crowd management contracts it also has agreements in place to provide a crowd control service to venues in London, Cardiff, Birmingham, Nottingham and Manchester. Current information on ShowSec International can be found at www.crowd-management.com.

Goldrange Ltd

Terry Wise and his wife Kathy formed Goldrange Ltd in 1983 (Wise 2006) and within the short space of five years the company quickly became established as a major player in the leisure security industry. The story of how the company came into being began at the Barbican Centre in London in 1981. It was here that Terry Wise acted as a consultant to the Centre during its final stages of construction. His role was to ensure best practice in terms of the provision of office services and the implementation of efficient maintenance procedures for all office accommodation.

During the final stage of construction the Centre naturally encouraged visits by prospective clients and some of these visits comprised a large number of people, therefore the venue needed to ensure a safe environment for visitors. An important aspect of a safe environment naturally included emergency evacuation procedures for all people on site. The venue had not employed staff for the specific purpose of crowd control at this point and Terry Wise accepted responsibility for designing a strategic plan to ensure the safety of visitors and to recruit casual staff necessary to implement the plan operationally. Anyone who knows Terry will also know that he never does things by half. He did not simply put staff in positions, he made sure that his team was disciplined, presented a good image and most importantly, every person received training for their role in crowd safety.

Terry Wise.

As the venue began to stage events it was natural that management would turn to him to provide a range of services to their clients. These services ranged from cloakroom attendants to event safety stewards, security staff and promotions people. It was very much a casual arrangement but, nevertheless, it was necessary to provide these services under a company banner. In discussions with The Barbican Centre over a possible trading name for the new venture, Barbican management casually mentioned that they saw the services that had so far been provided by the new company to date had been 'personnel plus'. This remark struck a cord with Terry and Kathy and Personnel Plus was registered and became the name used for early Barbican contracts. With the new company name Terry naturally went back to the Barbican Centre in order to obtain a more permanent contract and he was successful. When the venue opened the company provided the staff for exhibitions and conferences under an in-house contract agreement.

With the success of the Barbican contract it was time to think about a wider company marketing strategy. Terry and his wife Kathy decided to market their new company as able to provide a 'Golden Range' of services to their clients. They quickly discovered a problem however; it turned out that there was a clothing company in London's Petticoat Lane that was already trading as Goldrange. This company was now advertising several times a day on London commercial radio stations. Would they force them to change the name? A quick check however established that the clothing company had neglected to register their brand name and Terry and Kathy promptly registered Goldrange Ltd in 1983. With the rights to the name they felt that they were in control but, rather than take issue with the clothing company they decided that there was much more to be gained by allowing the name Goldrange to be heard by thousands of people daily on radio.

Personnel Plus became Goldrange Ltd on all future contracts providing a varied category of staff to the exhibition and conference industry. Terry was Head of Operations while Kathy managed administration from their home address assisted by Nicola her 16-year-old daughter. Nicola had at this point successfully completed training to become a beautician only to be told by Boots chemists, her then employer, that she was too young to work in that area of activity. Encouraged by her parents to join the business, Nicola resigned from Boots and joined the company. Once she was old enough (18), she began working at events, starting off as a Safety Steward. Nicola Wise went on to become a highly experienced crowd manager and event safety officer.

Terry had realised from the start of his new venture that established companies such as ShowSec dominated the provision of crowd management and crowd control services to concert events. Therefore, if he was to expand the company further, he needed to find new markets. Football clubs were notorious for employing unpaid fans to steward a home game. Consequently most stewards were more interested in what was happening on the pitch than the terraces. What Terry Wise saw in terms of safety standards did not impress him and he quickly realised that there might be a market for offering football clubs the sort of professional service he was currently providing to the Barbican Centre, and he set about marketing a professional stewarding service to football clubs in the London area.

In 1985 the disastrous fire at the Bradford City Football Club reinforced the message that crowd safety at football matches needed to be addressed and that the introduction of well trained, disciplined stewarding was needed as a matter of urgency. Goldrange had by now moved into bigger offices, and Nicola had gained experience and had the confidence to take on more responsibility. Kathy Wise was still the backbone of the company office management team, but as a busy mother she wished to gradually reduce her working role within the company. New staff were employed to take the roles of recruiting, vetting and training. The company had recognised the importance of proper training for all staff from day one and Terry was surprised when talking to football clubs that they did not have good systems in place at this point. Now Goldrange was rapidly gaining a wide reputation for providing disciplined, trained staff. Later, son James would join the company and, like Nicola, he started to learn how the business operated aged 16, then began working as a steward at the age of 18. James worked his way through the ranks to become a respected event manager.

By 1988 Goldrange had won contracts with Charlton Athletic, who were at that time playing their football at West Ham's ground, and in addition secured business with Millwall FC who played at the Old Den. The combined number of staff amounted to less than 50 people but it was an opening into a wider football market. Following the Hillsborough disaster, also in 1988 and the Taylor Report in January 1990, Goldrange found that more and more football clubs were interested in talking to them. Goldrange had begun by providing approximately 30 staff and was now providing approximately 600 on a regular basis. By the nineties the company was regularly providing well in excess of 1000 trained staff to a wide range of events.

Goldrange retained their contract with Charlton Athletic for over 11 years but a decision to terminate the contact was taken by Goldrange management following what they considered to be a breach of contract by the club. Goldrange claimed that the club consistently encouraged key members of Goldrange staff to leave their employment and work direct for the club. An independent investigation by a representative of the Football League subsequently found that Charlton AFC acted improperly and Goldrange were awarded a substantial compensation.

Over the next 20 years Goldrange claim to have provided staff for 99% of football clubs in and around the greater London area. They also provided literally hundreds of staff on a regular basis at all events at Wembley Stadium through to the time the Stadium closed, and was the In House Stewarding and Security Supplier to the Crystal Palace National Sports Centre and Athletics Stadium for over 15 years. A measure of their standing within sport events is demonstrated by the fact that Goldrange were the first stewarding contract organisation to become members of the Football Safety Officers Association (FSOA). In 1996 Goldrange were appointed the official supplier of Stewarding and Security staff to the Football Association. This contract commenced with the European Championships being held in this country and enabled Goldrange to continue with the FA right up to 2006, at which time the Wise family involvement with Goldrange finally came to an end.

In 2001 Goldrange Ltd merged with Reliance Security Services (RSS) who were at that time the one of the largest private security companies operating in the UK. Terry Wise continued as Managing Director (MD) until his contract ended in 2004. He was succeeded as MD by Nicola. James was the Operations Manager. Both Nicola and James resigned in 2005, however, to join Show & Event Security where they both hold senior positions at the time of writing. Terry Wise joined the Football Association where he works with the England football team as a member of the security team. Current information for Goldrange Security can be found at www.crowd-management.com.

Show & Event

In common with the majority of people who work in the leisure security industry, Tony Ball, Managing Director of Show and Event, found himself involved with events almost by accident. His career began in the mid eighties when he accepted casual employment with ShowSec at the Reggae Sunsplash presented by Capital Radio at the Crystal Palace Football Club. At the time Tony was a serving soldier and his intention was merely to work for one day at the event. Twenty-two years later he is running his own leisure security company.

Tony worked on a casual basis for ShowSec from 1984 until 1986 when the military posted him to Canada. On his return from Canada in 1987 he once again took up casual employment with ShowSec until he completed military service in 1988. At this point he accepted a full time managerial position with ShowSec at their London office. During his time at ShowSec Tony was quickly promoted, first to a senior managerial position as my assistant and subsequently to Operations Director.

It would be wrong of me to claim that I taught Tony Ball his job on the grounds that he acted as my assistant for a couple of years. For a person to reach the top of their profession that person must have an in-built instinct for the job and Tony has a natural ability to plan a major crowd management operation and he thrives on a challenge. A measure of his ability is the fact that in his first year at ShowSec he undertook to crowd manage 15 major outdoor concerts for Michael Jackson. Tony acted as the event controller at each show, which meant that he was directly responsible to me for tactical operations at every event. This was a tremendous responsibility for a person relatively new to the industry and it is to his credit that every show was managed without serious mishap.

Tony left ShowSec in 1998. His departure from the company bizarrely mirrored my own when I left Artistes Services. He was dissatisfied with the fact that Gerry Slater and I were considering selling the company and naturally he was unsure of his position. In simple terms, it was time to move on. Move on he did by forming Show & Event Security. Shortly after forming his own company, Tony was joined by Liam Wheatley who was also a graduate of the ShowSec training programme. Liam has been with Show & Event from the start and he continues to travel the world with the rich and famous.

Show & Event got off to a good start managing events thanks to Tony's reputation as a capable crowd manager. Not all his early ventures were successful however. In 1999 he undertook a crowd management contract for the eclipse in Devon. It was anticipated by the promoter that a huge crowd would turn up to witness the eclipse and watch the entertainment

The author and Ned Kelly (Special Forces) photographed whilst instructing on a close protection course.

Showsec International celebrity team: Dave Lindsay, Bob 'Emperor' Maxie, Paul Dalanegra, Simon Page and Michael Richardson.

Jackie Jackson, one of the few women civilian close protection officers at Showsec.

Receiving my Doctorate.

Jill McCracken, the first serving police officer to gain a Foundation Degree in Crowd Safety Management, receiving her degree from Chief Inspector Mark Canning (Hertfordshire Police).

Darren Edwards, chairman Safestyle Security.

Paul Brown (ex Royalty Protection) who worked at Showsec.

The great Nigel Browne who passed the entry criteria for 21 SAS but was sadly killed in a helicopter crash in America before he could take up his position.

provided, but unfortunately very few people bought tickets and the production company went into liquidation, with Show & Event owed a great deal of money. Undaunted, he pressed on to gain a contract for the V festival at Chelmsford the same year, which enabled him to start a climb back.

Since the year 2000 Show & Event have retained the Chelmsford V show contract. Other major event contracts undertaken include major events at Knebworth where the company managed three consecutive Robbie Williams shows totalling 375,000 people, part of the Live8 contract at Hyde Park and shows at Woburn and other green field sites.

An interesting observation with regard to Show & Event are the inroads the company has made into providing stewards for street events. In recent years the company has expanded their field of operations to include New Year's Eve celebrations and the Mayor's New Year's Day parade and various other street events in London. This type of event was previously regarded by the London Metropolitan Police to be a police role exclusively. In addition to street events, Tony was invited, in 2002, to crowd manage the first ever concert event presented in the grounds of Buckingham Palace and The Mall in honour of the golden jubilee of HM the Queen. At the time of writing (2006) Show & Event are involved in discussions to manage more street events. Current information on Show & Event can be found on the web at www.showandevent.com.

Olympus Security

Olympus Security is a leisure security company that took a single task, that of providing door staff, and developed a company by recognising a gap in what many people consider to be an over-crowded leisure security industry. Once again we see the recurring theme of individuals becoming involved in the leisure security almost by accident.

In 1998 Pat Strutt met socially with a friend who was at that time providing door supervisors to a couple of clubs in the Cheltenham area. In the course of their conversation this friend expressed the view that he needed help with his business administration. Pat agreed to provide assistance with office administration for a short term as he was, in his words, "*at a loose end at the time*". With limited capital company growth was naturally slow but nevertheless Pat felt that the business had potential. The basic problem was that his partner did not appear to share his view.

What was needed was a partner with security experience and ambition.

In 1999 a mutual friend introduced Pat Strutt to Peter Gauchi (known affectionately as 'the Brown Bear or Bear in Special Forces circles). Peter had previously acted as a Special Forces close quarter combat instructor; he had also trained the South Wales Police in self-defence. Prior to his meeting with Pat Strutt, Peter Gauchi had gained a reputation for reliability and professionalism on the celebrity protection circuit. He is a highly experienced VIP protection specialist. Peter was in fact a member of a team of Special Forces personnel that I put together to secure cash, protect integrity rights and protect VIPs at the first Donington Monsters of Rock that I managed as ShowSec. Following Donington, Peter undertook several contracts for ShowSec to protect international entertainment celebrities, until he decided to go freelance on the celebrity protection circuit.

As a result of their meeting in 1999, Peter joined Olympus with a brief to expand the company further into the leisure security market. The friend who had worked with Pat left to continue to work on club doors and Olympus became a partnership of Pat Strutt and Peter Gauchi. As Pat Strutt explained to me, *"the theory behind the Olympus partnership was to use Peter's contacts to obtain work in leisure security while he* (Pat) *provided company administration expertise.* The aim of the company initially was to gain regular contracts to pay salaries. A long-term aim, however, was to use these regular contracts to gain access to the lucrative celebrity close protection market.

To achieve the company aim Peter's strategy was to provide a guarding service to film and TV studios, which in turn would give the company access to production companies and performers. The first step was to obtain a contract with Leavesden Film Studios, which subsequently led to contracts to provide protection for the stars of the Harry Potter movies. Next, the company obtained a contract to provide guarding services at Elstree TV and film studios which led to a meeting with Endemol, the production company responsible for the highly successful Big Brother reality TV show. Olympus enhanced their reputation for professionalism when they foiled an attempt by the Fathers for Justice (F4J) movement to take over the Big Brother house at Elstree. This operation resulted in the arrest of 15 members of the F4J organisation. F4J had previously been very successful in occupying high profile buildings including Buckingham Palace and the House of Commons. The arrest of 15 of their members by Olympus led

The author and Gerry Slater receiving a crowd safety management award.

Showsec management team: Tony Ball, Yvonne Harrow, Bob Maxie, Jackie Jackson and Michael Richardson.

Group photo taken at the first ever Leisure Security meeting in Birmingham. Jim MacDonald is second left and Mark Hamilton on the extreme left.

The current Showsec management team: Steve Reynolds, Mark Harding, Richard Church, Simon Battersby and Roy Wise.

the leader of the F4J organisation to be quoted in the press as saying, *"The Palace should employ this security company (Olympus) as they are the only people that have stopped us so far"*.

Since that incident Olympus has worked on a regular basis for Endemol, providing guarding, crowd control and celebrity close protection services. A person who has played an important part in the development stage of Olympus is Nigel Jones. Nigel regularly manages contracts and events, particularly in Wales, where he is the area manager. In 2006 the company added Paul Gough to the management team. Paul holds a brief to manage the Olympus Security Industry Authority (SIA) approved lose protection (CP) training programme, in addition to managing operational CP contracts. You can find out more about Olympus at www.olympus-security.co.uk.

Special Events Security Ltd

This company was selected for inclusion in this chapter because of the impact that it has made on crowd safety standards at horse racing events. Once again this does not imply that this is the only area that the company operates in. As stated previously, all security companies today are compelled by a highly competitive market to be active in the provision of leisure security services to a wide range of events. Special Events Security Ltd has, however, established a reputation for service within racing circles, particularly at Ascot, Aintree and Cheltenham, where they have provided security and crowd control services for many years.

The company was formed in the late eighties by Dennis Hutchings and Mark Grant, two former members of the Household Division (The Guards). Both men were drawn to the private security industry initially simply as a means to earning a living as civilians, for as Mark Grant put it to me, *"there was not much of a requirement in the late 80's for former soldiers who were either weapons instructors, or tank commanders"*. The private security industry seemed to be a logical choice, therefore, for people who had received military training. The intention had been to take on security guarding contracts but Dennis Hutchings had worked on a casual basis for Artiste Services while still a serving soldier and it was perhaps this experience that influenced the partnership to focus on the provision of leisure security services.

As a new leisure security company it was difficult to compete with companies that had established a reputation over 20 years of providing services to event organisers, but the eighties was a time when 'rave' events were very popular. Established concert or event promoters did not generally promote these events. They were organised by a new breed of young entrepreneur that wished to cater for a new form of entertainment event. Dennis and Mark immediately saw an opportunity for business and they took advantage of it by providing security services to this new form of event that was promoted in warehouses, tents and fields.

The partnership realised, of course, that rave events were unlikely to last long before established promoters took them over and they would employ leisure security companies with whom they had long standing arrangements. This proved to be correct because raves quickly became mainstream 'dance' events promoted at permanent venues with in-house security teams. The challenge therefore was to capitalise on their crowd control expertise gained at raves to gain work at other forms of event. Once again we see the development of a new company coinciding with post Hillsborough and the publication of the Taylor Report, after the death of 96 people on 15th April 1989. The report identified staff training as a key requirement in a venue safety and security/stewarding plan. At that time training conducted by football clubs consisted mainly of a quick pre-match introduction with regard to staff duties such as, collecting tickets or cash on the gates or making sure that the gangway and aisles at a stadium where kept clear. Many football clubs found it difficult to recruit and train stewards in required numbers and, as we have already seen in the Goldrange review, this naturally opened up football to the leisure security industry. Like a number of other security companies, Special Event Security took advantage of the need for football clubs to move into that market.

Having established a company profile in terms of the provision of trained staff working under the direction of a disciplined management team, the company was now actively seeking other new markets. As we have already seen, however, it was difficult to break the dominance of other major companies in the concert market. Not surprisingly for two ex-cavalry soldiers, the partnership turned to horse racing to seek more business. Established leisure security companies had largely ignored racing but race meetings attracted very large crowds to some high profile meetings. Success came when the company was awarded a contract to provide security and crowd control teams to Ascot.

Crowd control at race meetings differs a good deal from crowd control at a concert or sport event for several reasons. Firstly, there will be crowd migration on a mass scale at a major meeting as punters move from at the end of a race to the bar, the toilets, the tote and then back to their viewing position to watch the next race. Secondly, there is obviously a need for the movement of horses through the crowd to the parade ring, onto the course and back to the enclosure at the end of a race. From a security point of view alcohol abuse can be a major problem at popular meetings particularly when people are celebrating a good win. Working at race meetings therefore requires a unique understanding of crowd psychology just as much as football or rock concerts.

The importance of understanding the psychology of a race crowd was to prove very useful on April 5th 1997 when the company provided over 300 security staff to Aintree for the Grand National. The event received a coded telephone warning that a bomb had been placed on the racecourse.

Peter 'The Bear' Gouchi with Elton John.

Merseyside Police advised that the code word was genuine and the racecourse management team should take the threat seriously. With no knowledge of where the device had been placed, the only safe option was to evacuate 78,000 people from the venue. Once the instruction had been given to evacuate, the total crowd was moved off of the racecourse, watched by an estimated ten million people live on television. Press reports quite justly claimed that the evacuation of 78,000 racegoers on that Saturday, carried out by a combined security and stewarding team, was a major achievement by anyone's standards, and was at that point possibly the largest evacuation of personnel carried out since the second world war. As Mark Grant put it to me, when discussing how smoothly the evacuation appeared to have taken place, *"my years of serving in the Army kicked in and it proved the old military adage – easy training hard combat, hard training easy combat"*.

The success of the evacuation operation on that day led to contracts for the company within many countries where horse racing and equine events are popular. The experience gained by the management team on that faithful Saturday back in 1997 has been built into staff training programmes to ensure improved quality of security and stewarding operations at racing events.

In 2007 Dennis Hutchings sold his interest in the Special Event Security to a major guarding company. Mark Grant, also a graduate of the BCUC Crowd safety Management FD programme continues to manage the company at the time of writing.

In terms of creating a specific leisure security industry, 1993 was arguably the first time that leading leisure security companies came together for the purpose of discussing a common approach to establishing an identity separate from man guarding. That year a conference was held at the Home Office Emergency Planning College, Easingwold, to discuss safety standards at social events. Most of the leading players attended and it was agreed that the issue of crowd safety needed formal recognition. The following year I organised what was billed as the Leisure Security Industry Conference, which was held at the Hyatt Hotel, Birmingham on the 5th October 1994. With considerable help from Jon (JC) Corbishly, the conference attracted a very good industry response. I opened the conference by introducing Stuart Galbraith, a leading UK concert promoter, who argued that if the industry did not get its act together, legislation would be introduced to force us to take measures that might be unsuitable. Other speakers raised issues that included tax compliance and health and safety. The conference then heard presentation from Sergeants Malcolm Ding and Ian Ellison from Essex Police, on the role of the police at events, and Raymond Clarke (S.I.T.O.), who advised the meeting on security industry training opportunities. The meeting was closed by Mark Hamilton from Rock Steady who urged the meeting to take on the challenge of training appropriate to industry needs.

In fairness it must be said that there was no dramatic change immediately. Change took several years. The first thing that happened was the formation of an association. This effort was short-lived however. Membership consisted of only a few companies and it was decided to reform as a branch of The Event Suppliers Association (TESA) in order to be a part of a larger organisation. This move proved to be a mistake, however, as crowd safety issues tended to get lost in a wide range of topics. Eventually Bert van Horck from Holland suggested that the United Kingdom Crowd Management Association (UKCMA) be formed along the lines of a successful Dutch model. The UKCMA was then formed under the chairmanship of Terry Wise (Goldrange), who steered it through the difficult period of the introduction of security licensing in the UK. Terry retired in 2007 and Mark Harding (ShowSec) was elected as chair. Mark has continued to develop close links with Buckinghamshire Chilterns University College (BCUC) in order to establish national training standards.

Harvey Goldsmith presenting me with a Lifetime Achievement Award from Total Production Magazine.

6 LEARNING FROM THE PAST

The expertise that exists today in terms of crowd safety management has been built on lessons learned from fatal accidents that have ranged from fires in theatres and clubs to crowd related disasters at concert and sports events. Fatal accidents have been the catalyst for published guidance in the UK; these guides and the accidents or incidents that brought them into being are reviewed in the next chapter. This chapter considers the cause and effect of two fatal incidents at rock concerts.

The first case study is that of a crowd crush in front of a stage at the 1988 Donington Monsters of Rock show which claimed the lives of two young men and injured an estimated 30 others. This accident was the catalyst for an upgrade of published guidance for concerts and live events. The accident provides valuable lessons for those involved with the planning for front of stage safety at modern day rock concerts at open-air venues. It is acknowledged here that the front of stage accident at the Roskilde Festival, Denmark, in 2000 claimed more lives (nine deaths) than Donington (two deaths). The Monsters of Rock Accident is detailed here simply because I was present at the time of the accident and therefore able to give a more 'first hand' account. Students of crowd safety are advised to find an account of the Roskilde accident on the web.

The second case study is that of an ingress failure at a concert held at Arad, Israel, on the 18th July 1995. A 16-year-old young woman and a 17-year-old young man died and many others were injured as a result of a crowd crush during ingress to the Atrock Rock Festival. Two days later a 15-year-old woman died as a result of injuries she received during the accident. The immediate response from some Israeli politicians was to call for a ban on all similar events. It is further acknowledged here that the 1979 Cincinnati disaster at the Riverfront Coliseum claimed more lives (11 deaths). However, this accident is well documented. My decision to include the Arad accident rather than Cincinnati is based on the fact that I was invited to Israel to advise on necessary safety measures at rock concert events. My account of the accident provided here is taken from a report that I submitted to the Israeli Concert Promoters Association. The logic applied here is that the student of crowd safety management planning can research and conduct comparative studies in order to establish the lessons that *should* have been learned.

Donington Monsters of Rock 1988

On the 28th August 1988 two young men died and a third was seriously injured and a number of others required medical attention in a crowd related incident during an open air rock concert billed as the 'Monsters of Rock' at the Donington Park motor race circuit in north west Leicestershire. This review of the accident is a personal account of my involvement in the crowd-related accident that happened on that day.

My involvement at the Monsters of Rock was as Head of Security and Crowd Management planning. At the time I was Chairman of ShowSec International Ltd., the company contracted by Aimcarve, the company responsible for promoting the event. I attended all pre-meetings and I had a good working knowledge of the site having worked on all events since 1980. For the 1988 event I was responsible for strategic planning prior to the concert, tactical and operational crowd management during the event, which included crisis management should the need arise, and all security matters.

The following is not claimed to be an account of every detail of what happened on that day, it is simply the recollections of one who was actually there. As with all accidents or incidents there will doubtless be other witness accounts from people who were present that day and who will recall things differently. This is natural when people see things from different perspectives. My version of the accident is, however, based on a broad view of the sequence of events and the benefit of radio reports to me from trained supervisors. From this wide perspective I believe my version presents an accurate account of the events that lead to the loss of two lives, the serious injury to one person and a traumatic experience for many other people who were involved either as victims or rescuers.

The incident at the 1988 Monsters of Rock concert has been the subject of much discussion by those that have an interest in crowd safety matters. At the time of the incident the media showed a natural interest as would be expected when two people die in such high profile circumstances. Unfortunately, much of what was reported by the press as the cause and effect of the incident was inaccurate. For example, the name of the act quoted in some reports as being on the stage at the time was the singer

David Lee Roth; it was in fact Guns 'n' Roses. Other reports indicated that a high crowd density build triggered the incident directly at the front of the stage subsequently causing crushing. This was also inaccurate. Several other papers claimed that the group on stage refused to stop playing; this again was inaccurate. Yet another report claimed that police were directly involved within the crowd at the time of the incident when in fact the police were not in the arena at all.

Confusion over what actually happened was possibly due to the fact that there had in fact been *three* separate incidents that day. Reporters were possibly unaware of this when they questioned people. Perhaps, confused by the different versions given by some witnesses, they (the press) simply cobbled together a version of a single incident. While this version may have satisfied newspaper editors it did little to help students of crowd safety to discover the true course of events.

Previous History of the Event

Promoter Maurice Jones, Chairman of Aimcarve Ltd, the concert organisers, first staged the Monsters of Rock in 1980. Jones enjoyed a well-earned reputation for promoting good rock shows. The 1980 show was an immediate success with rock fans. Many people travelled from different parts of Europe to be there. The demand for an annual rock show was clearly evident and the show was staged annually.

Heavy rock groups came to regard the Monsters of Rock show as being a major international showcase. To play at Donington was seen to be performing at *the* rock event in the heavy metal calendar. It was covered by virtually all the trade press, and in addition to being broadcast live on radio bands often filmed their performances for future video promotion to enhance a sales campaign of their latest recording.

Many fans travelled great distances to be there regardless of who was performing as the headline act. At the first concert in 1980 the demand for tickets was such that people arrived and set up camp on the Monday prior to Saturday's concert. Over the years the promoter actively discouraged camping and tried to present the event as a one-day concert not a festival. Nevertheless some fans still arrived with tents on the Friday evening. The promoter did provide facilities for these people. These facilities included toilets, lighting, large marquees (for those without tents), food vendors and vast amounts of firewood.

The campsite itself was an amazing prelude to a rock concert. Nobody appeared to want to sleep. There was perhaps what could only be described kindly as a *carnival atmosphere*. Rock fans have a well-deserved reputation for a love of alcohol and giving them the opportunity to spend all night in a field with a ready supply of beer while listening to ear splitting rock music appears to be their vision of heaven. In fact some of them had been known to enjoy the Friday night on the campsite so much that they have slept through the entire day of the concert and gone home on the Sunday having had a wonderful time!

The Venue

Donington Park is a motor race circuit situated approximately midway between Nottingham and Derby at the village of Castle Donington. The site itself is next to the East Midlands International airport. The circuit has a long history of motor sport and the track has been upgraded to handle F1. However it is perhaps best known as the home of the British Motor Cycle Grand Prix. Motor sport attracts large crowds and the venue has developed good working relationships with the emergency services. As one would expect there was, and still is, a major incident plan in place which takes into account virtually any scenario that could occur at a motor sport venue situated next door to a major airport.

Structural security is good. The venue is surrounded by a brick wall approximately twelve feet high topped with barbed wire. In 1988 entry and exit gates are designed to cope with ingress and egress crowds in the region of 200,000 people. The concert arena area is situated in the inner circle of the racetrack with a standing room area that could accommodate 150/200,000 people. In practical terms however this number of people could pose problems with sight lines for a concert, therefore attendance at the Monsters event would normally range from 50/100,000. Attendance for the 1988 event was given by the promoter as 85,000 people.

The stage was built at the north east corner of the arena, facing approximately south east so as to direct PA sound away from the village of Castle Donington and toward the open area of the nearby airport. In 1988 the grass area immediately in front of the stage sloped down toward the stage at a gradient of approximately 1/20. At the time this was considered advantageous to viewing, however after the incident this area was laid flat.

The Police

The police attended all Safety Advisory Group (SAG) planning meetings prior to the event but no police officers were present within the concert arena during the show. The police were fully advised of what was taking place during the event via radio communication but they did not take an active part in containing any of what turned out to be three separate incidents that took place, or the subsequent rescue operation of the injured. These actions were entirely the responsibility of ShowSec International Limited.

As stated previously, I had been present at every Donington concert from 1980 and I have never seen a serious confrontation between the police and the fans. The police had always adopted what I would describe as a realistic approach to the event. This is not to suggest that they ignored crime. Local officers have come to understand rock culture and they realised that a torn denim or leather look of the average rock fan did not signify that they were a rioting mob. All police control vehicles, temporary police station and facilities were therefore positioned near the main entrance to the site and not in the arena.

Officers did patrol the campsite during the evening and throughout the night of Friday but the event itself was left in the hands of a private security company employed by the promoter. The only officers in the arena in 1988 were two who were assigned as liaison officers and they were in the back stage area. In my opinion, the working relationship between private security and all the emergency services prior to 1988 were good.

Pre-Planning

The Public Entertainment License (PEL) for the event was issued by North West Leicestershire District Council who chaired regular meetings for some six months prior to the event. During the months leading up to the concert the local authority arranged a number of meetings with a Safety Advisory Group (SAG). SAGs are normally comprised of officers from the local authority, representatives from each of the emergency services, St. John Ambulance and other interested parties such as traffic management and health and safety. The promoter is naturally expected to attend. For the SAG meetings that took place in 1988 both myself and Tony Ball, who at that time was my assistant and would act as the site controller on the show, attended all meetings. For Tony and I, however, planning for the 1988 concert actually began earlier in March of that year with informal meetings with the promoter. At this point we were advised that Iron Maiden would be the headline act. This particular act had a long history of successful events and the indications were that they would attract a large crowd but their stage act was unlikely to cause serious problems.

Subsequently we were advised that a crowd attendance of 85,000 people was likely. In order to maintain good sight lines for this number of people the promoter agreed to provide large daylight vision screens each side of the stage to avoid crushing at the centre of the crowd mass. A single primary barrier constructed of scaffold and ply board was installed for the event. This design was common at the time. The event used only one stage. In 1988 there was no established practice to set up an Emergency Liaison Team (ELT) comprised of local authority officers to monitor the event, therefore this event did not have one.

On completion of a site survey I proposed that a total of 520 steward staff be deployed on the day and all parties agreed this number. In July we were advised that the line-up of major artistes for the concert was to be:

> Iron Maiden
> KISS
> David Lee Roth
> Guns 'n' Roses

I had worked previously with three of the four named acts and they were considered to be low risk in terms of crowd behaviour. However the fourth act, Guns 'n' Roses, were a new young American act that I knew little of. Our risk assessment indicated that their stage act was aggressive in style and that they had strong record sales that would possibly attract a large number of their own fans to the show. Our audience profile indicated that these fans would be younger and more volatile than we would normally expect. The term used to describe this new trend in heavy rock was *Thrash Metal*. This title was given to indicate the way that these fans thrashed about wildly to the music to a point where they appeared to be hitting each other. As a result of our risk analysis we increased the number of security staff in the front of stage pit to 40.

The Show
The weather conditions prior to the concert were bad. It rained continuously from the Monday to the Thursday. Nevertheless the crew completed

construction of the site on time. By Friday the weather had improved but conditions were still very wet and it was necessary to impose restrictions on vehicle movement around the site. On Saturday, the day of the concert, the weather remained overcast with occasional showers.

The doors opened to the public at 08:00hrs and ingress was completed without incident. Those fans who had arrived early made their way directly to the front of stage where security staff were not able to get them to sit them down due to the wet ground conditions. However the crowd was cheerful and friendly and appeared to be happy to wait until the supporting acts would start to appear. During the period of their wait recorded music was provided by a disc jockey from BBC radio.

Incident #1

At 1300hrs the control room received a message from the backstage supervisor advising that high winds were causing a serious problem to the daylight screen positioned at stage right. A rigging crew was alerted and I arranged to meet with Tony Ball at that location to assess the situation. By the time we reached the location however, the complete screen assembly had collapsed and was only prevented from falling onto a section of the crowd by a steel fence that surrounded the backstage area.

The ShowSec supervisor had moved the crowd from the danger area and a rigging crew was attempting to retrieve the damaged screen. Efforts by the rigging crew were continuously frustrated at this time, as a small section of the crowd insisted on attempting to stand underneath the suspended rig because the screen was still relaying live pictures of the act on stage. Their actions, however, put them in great danger. My actions at this point were to deploy more staff from the pit to secure the danger area, cut the power to the screen and secure the damaged screen so that it would not fall. It was not necessary to stop the show as the band on stage shortly finished their act. The team operation to retrieve the screen took approximately one hour but before it was finally completed Guns 'n Roses went on stage. Almost immediately I received a report from the pit supervisor that there was an unusually high level of crowd activity taking place in front of the stage. At this point I detailed a security team to return to the pit. I remained at the screen location to ensure that it was safe and I detailed my assistant, Tony Ball, to go to the pit and send me a situation report.

Incident #2

At approximately 1415 hrs Tony Ball called me on the radio and asked for me to come to the pit in front of the stage urgently. I immediately went to the area which was approximately one hundred yards from where I was. On arrival at the pit I saw that there was a great deal of activity within the crowd. Density was clearly at 0.3 (3 persons per m^2) immediately in front of the barrier but this did not appear to be a serious problem. At approximately ten rows back, however, a density of approximately $0.5m^2$ (2 persons per m^2) allowed room for lateral surges which was becoming a problem. I witnessed lateral crowd surges that ran across the complete front of the stage. One particular surge started at stage right and stopped suddenly with a crowd collapse at the centre approximately 15 yards out from the front of stage. It was immediately obvious that this was a serious situation as approximately 50 people were involved. I sent a four-man team into the crowd to assist and assess the problem. At the same time I sent a message to the stage to ask the singer with Guns 'n' Roses to stop the show as we had a serious problem. The singer immediately stopped the show and he then used the stage PA to calm the crowd and advise them of the problem.

The advance team reached the spot and attempted to send back a radio message but unfortunately their communications failed due to the fact that victims of the incident grabbed at their radios and pulled the microphone lead out. At this point the team leader signalled to me to go to the spot. I instructed Tony Ball to remain in charge of the pit and I advised the control room, which was managed by my business partner Gerry Slater, that I was going out into the crowd with another team. The show was still stopped at this point.

On reaching the spot I found that the advance team was still dealing with approximately 10-15 people who had obviously been at the bottom of a crowd collapse. Ground conditions were bad and the people involved were covered in mud, I decided that they should all be extracted from the crowd for their own safety. We managed to lift most people up and were passing them toward the pit when unfortunately the band on stage assumed that the incident had been fully contained and they resumed playing. Suddenly, the whole crowd around us erupted. A large section of the crowd, and two of our own security team, collapsed in front of us. I witnessed approximately 30/35 bodies that suddenly piled up in front of me covered in mud. Our efforts to pull people off of the pile were hampered by the fact that people behind us climbed onto our backs in an attempt to, what we now know, be crowd surfing. In some cases these people dived over our heads onto the pile of bodies.

At this point I lost communications as my radio and earpiece was ripped from me. Consequently I was not able to advise Tony of the situation. He realised, however, that we were in serious trouble and he quickly dispatched another ten-man team to assist us. At the same time he stopped the show for the second time. Once assistance reached us I was able to establish a cordon around the scene and retrieve the bodies. Tony then managed to establish a line of security people that extended from the pit to us and this enabled us to pass people back to St. John Ambulance staff who were stationed at stage right. We managed to retrieve over 30 people, all of whom were covered in mud. It was noticeable that some were also bleeding and others had obviously vomited. When we reached the bottom of the pile we discovered one person unconscious. This person was immediately passed to the pit where he was resuscitated by Steve Johnson, a ShowSec pit team member.

Unfortunately, as we removed what we took to be the last casualties we discovered another two bodies underneath them. These two were both laying face down in about four inches of mud and they were almost covered over. At first I did not realise that they were people. The pressure load on these two victims was such that we had to dig under them with our bare hands to turn them over. We managed to extract both of them from the mud but they appeared to us to be lifeless. Suddenly the band started to play again and crowd conditions made it impossible for us to examine them in any detail. We immediately evacuated the victims to St. John where they were removed to hospital but, tragically, were found to be dead on arrival.

Two senior police officers, who had been advised of the seriousness of the incident, arrived at the scene. The first indications were that the police wanted to stop the concert. After further discussions with the promoter, however, the show was allowed to continue as the police then decided that no purpose would be served by stopping the event. It was agreed, in fact, that there might be a risk to public order by doing so as the majority of the audience were not aware of the seriousness of the incident.

Incident #3

At 1700hrs David Lee Roth was on stage. Both Tony Ball and myself had remained in the pit area to monitor the crowd. There had been no further incidents since Guns 'n' Roses had finished their set but we had decided to remain in the area. At approximately 17:15hrs I noticed a young woman, stage right about ten yards out, who appeared to feint. She disappeared from my view and she did not reappear. As I was the only person who knew exactly where she was, I advised the team that I was going in to find her. I went into the crowd and on arriving at the spot I found a young woman aged approximately 15 laying face down on the ground. The crowd parted and I was able to check her condition; she was still breathing, there was a pulse and there were no obvious signs of injury. As she would have been in danger where she was, I lifted her up to take her back to the pit, where a medical team could attended to her. At this point the pit team signalled to the crowd to part to allow me room to bring her in and I started to do so.

As I approached the pit I noticed one member of the pit team begin to climb the front of the stage. I can only assume that he was in a state of shock from the earlier incident, because he climbed onto the stage and pleaded with David Lee Roth to halt the show as there had been too many injuries and the show should be abandoned. The singer, not realising the fact that he was a member of the pit team, assumed he was about to be attacked and called his two personal bodyguards onto the stage. They promptly grabbed hold of our man and literally threw him off the stage into the pit. Some sections of the crowd had realised what was happening took offence at this, and a dynamic surge toward the stage occurred. It was possibly this incident that the press later mistakenly reported as being the point where Le Roth refused to stop the show.

At this point I was still in the crowd with the young woman in my arms. A member of the crowd, presumably seeing my security shirt, then decided that all security staff should be attacked and he hit me in the face with a one-litre plastic bottle even though I was obviously carrying a casualty. Although the bottle was only half full he hit me with enough force to knock me sideways onto the ground. This happened near to the barrier and fortunately the pit team was able to grab the young woman and I suffered the indignity of being rescued by my own pit team. The team also managed to recover our shell-shocked security man, who had actually missed the pit and landed in the crowd. He was also taken to St. John where he made a full recovery.

There were no further incidents, Iron Maiden completed their set and the show closed on time.

The Inquest

The inquest into the two deaths at Donington was held at Loughborough Town Hall during February 1989. After four days of listening to testimony from more than 30 people who were involved in the incident, the verdict reached was accidental death. The coroner praised the efforts by the pit team by saying *"their efforts undoubtedly saved lives"*.

The Aftermath

The sense of shock resulting from the Donington disaster was the catalyst for a review of the 1974 Greater London Council (GLC.) Guidance for pop concerts, which was used as a terms of reference at the time. A review body chaired by Richard Limb from the North West Leicestershire District Council invited members of the Concert Promoters Association, private security companies and volunteer groups to work with local authority officers and the emergency services throughout 1989/90 to formulate a new guidance document for concert events. The result was the *Guide to Health, Safety and Welfare at Pop Concerts and Similar Events*. Perhaps more commonly referred to by the colour of its cover as, 'The Purple Guide'. The front cover of which had a photograph taken of a crowd at a later Monster of Rock concert. I was pleased to have had input into the document in the form of the chapter on crowd management.

The Purple Guide was also significant in that it advocated that an Emergency Liaison Team (ELT) should be established for each major concert event. The ELT should be made up from members of the emergency services, the local authority and the security team. The role of the ELT is to immediately take command if a serious incident occurred, the police officer present would then take control of evacuation if necessary. The system is now standard practice in the UK. Published guidance is the subject of the next chapter.

Disaster at the Atrock Festival

Shortly after the fatal accident at Arad that claimed the lives of three young people, I was contacted by concert promoter Yahuda Talit from Talit Productions based in Israel. Mr. Talit was not involved with the Arad concert at all. He contacted me on behalf of the Israeli Concert Promoters Association (ICPA). The ICPA invited me to go to Israel to make an independent assessment of the disaster, the primary purpose of the visit being to identify the root cause(s) and suggest ways of improving public safety at future concert events. I accepted the invitation on condition that no fee should be paid to me, as my report must represent a truly independent opinion. I had no interest in finding excuses for badly promoted shows. I also insisted that my findings should be made freely available to the official government inquiry team if they wished to read it and that I would be allowed to speak freely to the press if interviewed. These terms were accepted unconditionally by the ICPA and I arrived in Israel on Sunday 6th August 1995, just over one month after the fatal accident. The following account of my visit to Israel is taken from notes written at the time. Unfortunately the original report was lost due to a computer failure. To the best of my knowledge, however, this account reflects an accurate summary of my visit and subsequent conclusions.

On my arrival in Israel I was advised that a meeting had been arranged with the ICPA membership that evening. At this meeting concert promoters explained their method of approach to safety planning. The approach to safety standards basically followed the system applied in the UK. Unfortunately the Atrock Festival promoter was not a member of the ICPA and was not available for interview. Consequently it was not possible to establish how crowd safety standards were planned for Atrock. Initially I gained information from press reports regarding the accident. Press reports of the tragedy had been translated into English for me and I was able to have access to press photographs. I was advised that two official enquiries had been conducted into the incident, one by the police and a second by the Education and Culture Committee. The ICPA, however, did not have copies of these reports.

I contacted the police and requested a copy of their report but I was advised that it was marked *secret* and therefore not open for inspection by anyone, not even relatives of the victims. The reason for secrecy was not explained. Interviews with individual police officers involved with the event were, however, permitted and given freely. The conclusions of the Education and Culture Committee had not been finally reached, therefore it was not possible to have a copy of their report either. I did manage to interview private security staff who worked at the event and members of the public who claimed to have attended the concert. These interviews combined with press reports and a site visit did enable me to build up a picture of what actually happened on the 18th July.

The Concert

Arad is a small town in southern Israel approximately 15mins drive from the Dead Sea. For 12 years prior to the 1995 event the town council, under the direction of the mayor, promoted the Arad Festival. Each year the complete town was given over to performers and artistes to stage drama, poetry, mime, street theatre and music. The festival lasts for a full four days and ran continuously 24 hours a day. As a performance of one type concludes so an alternative performance began at a different venue or location. A trip to Arad for the festival had become traditional for young Israelies and foreign visitors to the country.

After the 1991 festival it was decided to allow a commercial promoter to take on the specific task of presenting concerts for youth culture. Accordingly, the council brought in the Forum Company to stage contemporary rock and/or pop events. Forum was chosen because of their reputation as operators of popular discos. They had also been involved in the promotion of smaller live music events. The added attraction of rock to the festival appears to have worked well during 1992/3/4. During this period there seems to have been little cause for concern to the council, although the major rock promoters in Israel stated at my meeting with the ICPA that they had been concerned over safety standards following the 1994 event. Exactly why the promoters were concerned was not made clear by them, it was simply stated that they felt that crowd safety management was lacking. The ICPA did not voice their concern to any official body, it appeared to be confined to informal association meeting discussion.

By 1995 Forum had graduated from small events to promoting major concerts when they announced their intention to promote the American rock band R.E.M. at the sports stadium in Tel Aviv, although this concert was not actually scheduled until three weeks after the Arad festival. Nevertheless the company appears to have felt sufficiently confident to promote the Arad Festival event. The 1995 show was planned to be bigger and better than anything they had done previously. To ensure working capital they took on two brothers by the name of Schwartz and together they secured an open field site that was approved for a capacity of 18,000 people. Capacity attendance appeared to be based on the UK principle of 0.5m² (two persons per square metre).

As a temporary site the promoters needed to fence off the required area and this they did by erecting an 8ft high temporary wire mesh fence. The fence was supported at the base by standing each panel in concrete base blocks. Each panel is then linked to the next by inserting horseshoe type clips into the top of the hollow tubes of each panel. This type of fence is in common use at building sites and events held at temporary sites throughout Europe but it is not designed to take a pressure load without any form of bracing. No person interviewed was aware of bracing having been used at Arad.

Entry to the site for the public was via *one entrance only.* Staff supplied by a private security company controlled this entry gate. Police officers were also in attendance at the gate in some considerable number and they had complete authority to take on the spot decisions in all matters both inside and outside of the site. It was interesting to note during interviews with police officers that every one of them insisted that *they* had final responsibility for public safety matters *not* the private security company. The attitude of the police was perhaps shaped by the volatile political situation that existed in Israel at that time. Terrorist attacks were common then, and still are today in Israel.

To ensure that people without tickets did not attempt to gain entry by climbing over the fence the promoters appear to have taken the decision to fix barbed wire at the top of each panel. The decision to install the wire could perhaps have been regarded by the organisers as a visible deterrent because, as stated previously, this type of temporary fence will not take the pressure load imposed by a single person let alone a crowd intent on seeing a free show. Although the local police claimed responsibility for public safety they did not appear to be aware of the weaknesses of this particular type of fence installation and they did not object to it at the planning stage.

Event Marketing

The festival was billed as a presentation of three days of rock music to be held on the evenings of 18th, 19th and 20th of July 1995. Customers could purchase a one-event ticket for sixty-shekels (approximately £20) or by purchasing a three-day ticket for which customers would be entitled to a discount. To ensure that events are not over sold Israeli law required that a licensed ticket agency handle the distribution of all tickets sold. On this occasion the Hadran Agency based in Tel Aviv handled sales. Tickets for the three-day event sold well and there was a particularly heavy demand for the first concert on the 18th. This show was billed as the farewell performance by Israel's top rock group Machina. Possibly unknown to European audiences, Machina had dominated rock sales charts in Israel for the past 12 years. Demand to see their last performance was such that this particular show sold out quickly.

An important factor in marketing of the festival is that the promoters reached a private agreement with local banks. Under this agreement any person that opened a bank account with a minimum deposit of 30 shekels (£10), would receive a voucher that could be exchanged for a reduced price single day ticket. This offer was subject to availability of tickets on any particular day at the box office and *did not* guarantee a ticket. Many young Israeli's however mistakenly took this marketing campaign to be an offer of a single day ticket at a reduced price. In short, they thought that they had purchased a ticket for any of the three days of the event. Not surprisingly many young people rushed to open bank accounts in order to get a voucher. Very few people appear to have read the small print on the back of the voucher. Literally hundreds of young people now held what they firmly believed to be a ticket for a show that was already widely known to be sold out, when in fact what they held was a conditional voucher that did not guarantee entry to the event. Subsequently a great many voucher holders turned up on the 18th expecting to get in.

The Incident

Doors opened to the public at 20:45hrs. The opening of the doors was dictated by the length of time taken for the sound check of those groups that were appearing. Sound checks are necessary to establish a correct balance for the artiste and to enable the sound engineer to set his/her control panels for light and sound for each act. This particular sound check appears to have taken a great deal longer than most as it was not completed until 20:30hrs. The key factor in this case is that the first act was due to appear on stage at 21:00hrs. This time frame indicates that only *fifteen minutes* was allowed from the gates opening for the public to enter and the first act appearing on stage.

Witnesses stated to me that at the time gates were opened there was a large crowd, estimated in thousands, waiting to get in. With only *one entry gate* in use it was highly unlikely that more than a few hundred could have been admitted in time for the opening of the concert. Although the first act was not the headline act the sound of live music being heard by those on the outside was bound to cause crowd control problems for the security staff. A normal admission time for this size attendance would be expected to take in the region of two hours, however this is largely dependent on the number and location of ingress gates.

Interviewees stated that there were approximately 20 private security guards at the entry gate backed up by ten or 12 police officers. Neither appears to have coped effectively with the initial opening rush. Reports suggest that there was little attempt at establishing a linear queue pattern and bulk queuing quickly formed at the gate. A bulk queue situation was allowed to grow out of control for the next 45 minutes as security and police made frantic efforts to get as many people as possible through the gate.

Security staff interviewed stated that they had not been made aware of the likelihood of people turning up with vouchers and expecting to gain entry. When this did happen they (security staff) attempted to turn them away fearing they had found forged tickets, or at best referred them to the box office, which had sold out of tickets for that show. With so many people arriving with vouchers, the gate soon became totally blocked with people refusing to move until they had exchanged their voucher for a ticket. Those people with tickets then became very frustrated by the fact that they could hear that the show had begun but could not get in.

At 21:45hrs a police officer appears to have became so concerned over the situation at the gate that he took it upon himself to go to the stage and ask the support group to stop playing. The group stopped playing and the police officer left the stage. After waiting a short while and with no further information given to them, however, the group began to play again. After two songs it was made known to the group that there was a serious problem on site and they stopped for the second time. This time they left the stage. At 22:00hrs the police officer in charge at the site gave instructions to close the gate because he was afraid that the site would become overcrowded. A combined team of police officers and security staff then closed the gate.

Once the gate was closed the pressure from the crowd on the outside built up to a point where a lateral surge was spontaneously triggered onto the perimeter fence which then collapsed taking with it the closed gate. The fence fell inward onto a section of the crowd on the inside trapping them underneath it. This sudden pressure release carried people from outside to inside like a tidal wave. As people were carried forward they trampled over the ones trapped underneath the collapsed fence. Those underneath were not able to lift the fence due to the weight on top of them. Others close to what had been the top of the fence were trapped by the barbed wire fixed to each panel and of course, the panels were linked together.

Once the combined security and police team was able to establish control it was quickly realised that two people were dead and many injured. The show was then cancelled that night. Press reports of the incident claim that it took three hours to clear casualties from the site to hospital. Two days later the news was announced that a third person had died as a result of her injuries. Attempts were made to stage the remaining two shows but the artistes refused to take part and these shows were then cancelled.

Aftermath
According to information provided by the Israeli Concert Promoters Association the police officer in charge of the event was dismissed immediately after the accident and the area police chief posted to another area. It was not possible to interview these two officers, therefore it is not claimed here to be a fact. If disciplinary action was taken against these officers immediately, however, it would appear that action was taken before either of the two subsequent independent inquiries had even began. If accurate, the actions of the police are puzzling to say the least.

Interviews with individual officers led me to understand that the Israeli police do not train officers of any rank in proactive crowd management. This is by no means rare. I have never discovered a police force in any country that I have worked in to provide crowd management training; all train for crowd control. By setting themselves up as *the* authority on site, however, the Israeli police actually set themselves up to be competent crowd managers.

Private Security
Interviews with security staff in Israel revealed that formal training in proactive crowd management strategies was not a condition of their

licence to work. All of the persons interviewed (eight) claimed that their experience of working with concert crowds gave them an advantage over police officers but nevertheless they were not invited, or permitted, to advise the police on such issues.

Conclusions

The findings presented on two case studies here should not be misinterpreted to be simply a British or an Israeli problem. My study of concert safety standards leads me to believe that the failures found in both countries can still be found in other countries today.

It is common for the media to report that a crowd related fatal incident occurred as a result of panic or irrational crowd behaviour when crowd surge activity is the root cause. A crowd surge does not respect direction. It will occur directionally or laterally. The more dangerous of the two is the *lateral surge* as occurred at Donington because people are more likely to trip and fall over. They are then likely to be crushed to death by a vertical load imposed by a crowd collapse. A *dynamic surge* can begin when a crowd begins to ebb and flow. Where the surge hits an immovable object such as a closed gate or wall it will convert to a static pressure load.

The Donington accident was widely regarded at the time to have been caused by cultural activity, when in fact there were a number of factors that must be considered. These considerations must include crowd density, natural laws of crowd dynamics, front of stage barrier systems, venue design and staff training.

The tragedy at Arad was widely regarded at the time to have been caused by people trying to gain free entry to a sold out show. The decision on ingress facility design and fence type for an event that was known to have sold out 18,000 tickets in advance appears to indicate a lack of knowledge of pedestrian flow planning. The fixing of barbed wire to prevent non-ticket holders gaining entry actually indicates that those in charge of the production possibly suspected those problems could occur that night. In which case measures might have been taken to brace the whole fence line and install at least two more ingress gates.

No ingress flow calculations were available from the promoter, the police or private security at Arad therefore it is not known how the organisers considered design for crowd safety in terms of pedestrian flow.

Once again there were a number of important factors that should have been taken into consideration at the planning stage. These factors include queue management theory, pedestrian flow calculation, contingency planning, systems design (perimeter fence and ingress system), event marketing strategy, staff training, role of the police, communications and risk analysis, risk assessment and risk management.

The key factor in crowd safety planning is the risk analysis process, which requires the appointed crowd manager to undertake research into the cause and effect of any accident or incident that has occurred at an event similar to that which they are currently planning. The subject of risk as applied to events is covered in more detail in Chapter 8.

7 GUIDANCE AND LEGISLATION

Incidents and accidents such as those referred to in the last chapter have been the catalyst for a series of guidance documents published in the UK to aid event organisers and venue operators to plan for safe events. A tremendous amount of material has been published offering advice on the subject of crowd safety and security at events and this chapter has chosen to separate advice from guidance. It is reasoned here that advice can be accepted or ignored whereas guidance published by a government agency amounts to a set of rules that practitioners would be extremely unwise to ignore. Only guidance published by government agencies is therefore considered here.

Following a review of guidance, this chapter moves on to consider current legalisation introduced in the UK to regulate the security industry generally. The impact of the Security Industry Authority (SIA) licensing programme has had on leisure security is then considered in terms of its effect on safety standards at social events.

Published Guidance

A number of guidance documents have been published to assist event organisers and local authority officers to introduce a safety culture. These documents have often, but not always, been published as the result of an official inquiry into a serious or fatal incident. Guidance documents are now available that are specific to sports grounds, pop concerts and fire control within entertainment venues.

The manner in which local authority officers interpret guidance can have a marked influence on the organiser's attitude to safety planning. With over 600 local authorities currently in being in the United Kingdom, however, there are bound to be different shades of opinion among local authority officers as to how guidance is interpreted. The inexperienced officer might feel inclined to stick rigidly to the written word while the experienced officer may choose to use guidance as it was intended, purely as a guide. Alternatively, officers may opt to rely entirely on their personal experience.

Guide to Safety at Sports Grounds

Although this document has no statutory force, many of its recommendations are mandatory at individual grounds due to their inclusion in Safety Certificates issued under the Safety at Sports Grounds Act 1975, or the Fire Safety and Safety of Places of Sport Act 1987.

In the introduction notes the guide advises us that measures for improving the safety of spectators at sports grounds first became available following the Wheatley Report on crowd safety at sports grounds in 1972. This report had been submitted by the Rt. Hon Lord Wheatley at the request of the Secretary of State for the Home Department at the time and the Secretary of State for Scotland. This inquiry was set up following a serious accident on a stairway at Ibrox football ground in 1971 in which 66 people lost their lives in an accident on the Cairnlea Drive stair system (stair 13).

The staircase accident was not the first incident at Ibrox. Data provided by Elliot *et al* (1997) revealed that there had been two serious accidents previously on stair 13. In 1967 eight people were injured and in 1969 24 were injured in accidents. It would appear to people of a suspicious mind that stair 13 was appropriately numbered.

In his study of football disasters published under the title 'Catastrophes and Disasters', Smith (1992) explains how the 1971 accident happened at a match between Rangers and Celtic. The two teams traditionally play each other in a New Year fixture. Support for Rangers is traditionally drawn from the protestant community and Celtic from catholic areas. Consequently, there are underlying sectarian tensions. Games are normally played alternately at Ibrox (Rangers ground) and Park Head (Celtic).

There appears to be a general agreement by researchers with regard to the events leading to the accident that happened in January 1971 at Ibrox. For example Smith's published account of the accident tallies with an account by Robins (1990) published under the title, 'The World's Greatest Disasters Football Tragedies. Both researchers agree that with only a few minutes left to play Celtic were leading and Rangers fans, resigned to defeat, were leaving the ground in large numbers. Suddenly, Colin Stein equalised for Rangers and a roar went up from the crowd. People leaving by the Cairnlea Drive exit heard the roar and some of them attempted to return back up the stairs to see what had happened. The subsequent cross flow that resulted in someone falling over which then caused a crowd collapse.

Smith suggests that some reports indicate that a small boy was the first person to trip, however there is no clear evidence to support that theory. Records show that 66 people died and 200 were injured in the incident. Ironically, the Cairnlea Drive exit had been redesigned to allow safer crowd flow following the 1961 incident. Two additional platform levels had been installed on the stairway as a result of 1961. These were intended to break what was considered a steep descent but it would appear that nobody had considered the possibility that the crowd would suddenly wish to return *up* the stairs against the flow of those leaving. Pedestrian systems at Ibrox have since been completely redesigned. This is now all seated and capacity has been reduced. Today Ibrox is regarded as one of the most modern grounds in Europe.

The green guide is updated and reissued following any serious incident or problem. During 1976 it was revised to take into account the recommendations of a Working Party set up to study crowd behaviour. A further edition followed the Bradford fire in 1986, and again following the Taylor Report into the Hillsborough disaster in 1997. At the time of writing it is being considered for a rewrite, thankfully it would appear that this time a new edition is not prompted by a crowd related accident.

Fire Precautions in Places of Public Entertainment and Like Premises

The Guide to Fire Precautions in Existing Places of Entertainment and Like Premises is aimed primarily at indoor venues. Once again a document is generally referred to by the distinctive colour of its front cover, as the 'Yellow or Primrose guide'. The guide offers practical advice on fire control at clubs, pubs and theatres and within temporary structures (marquees). The guidance that is offered has been gained from data obtained by academic and fire service research into entertainment venue fires that have occurred over many years. Expert advice is provided on fire control and the use of fire extinguishers that is relevant to any type of venue. The document also contains important advice relevant to the calculation of pedestrian flow and crowd density.

Today our knowledge of the effects of fire and toxic smoke and new improved building materials has reduced the risk of fire at entertainment venues. Using non-combustible materials, methods of extracting smoke, and staff education, has therefore made venues safer. However, the '*one off*' 'indoor 'theme' event continues to present high risk. The Christmas and New Year period is an example of sensible fire precautions often being ignored for the sake of creating a carnival mood. Venue operators will hang flammable decorations from the ceiling and walls and reduce lighting levels in an effort to create 'an atmosphere' that will draw crowds. The temptation to overcrowd a venue for additional profit may also be a factor at these times.

It is popularly believed that a very serious fire at the Summerland leisure complex on the Isle of Man in 1974 prompted the guide. This fire had cost the lives of 50 people and caused the Governor of the island to set up a commission to investigate the cause (Fire Prevention No 158). The fire would have undoubtedly sent shock waves through the entertainment industry and caused many venue operators to review their fire safety procedures. It was, however, a fire at the Stardust Disco, Dublin, Eire in 1981 that proved to be the catalyst for official guidance specifically designed to take into account precautions for fire control at entertainment venues, first published in the UK in 1990.

The findings of the Isle of Man commission on the Summerland fire were drawn to the attention of all local authorities in a document issued jointly by the Home Office and the Fire Service in March 1975. The information contained in the joint Home Office and Fire Service circulars of 1975 had been studied by the Irish authorities and passed to their local authorities. However, the warnings were not heeded by all venues. The Stardust disco in Dublin was one such venue. Fire Prevention Report No 158 explains that in the early hours of Saturday 14 February 1981, during a St. Valentines dance, fire swept through the venue killing 48 people and injuring 128.

From discovery, to the fire beginning to diminish, was a mere 20 minutes. The then Irish prime minister, Mr. Charles Haughey, ordered a Public Inquiry. The enquiry team found that the fire was probably started deliberately by the ignition of upholstered seating, which it was alleged had been slashed to expose the polyurethane foam. The Inquiry subsequently found that the tragedy resulted from a combination of combustible furniture and fittings, inadequate structural fire protection, inadequate fire-fighting equipment and staff not trained in its use, lack of a plan of action in the event of fire and locked and obstructed fire exits. All of these points had been listed as relevant factors in the Summerland fire of 1974.

Immediately following the Stardust disco fire the Home Office, Scottish Office, and what was then the Health Department, set up a joint working party to consider the implications to venues in the U.K. The result of the working party findings was the Guide to Fire Precautions in Existing Places of Entertainment and Like Premises. The document is directed mainly at the professional or technically trained officers in local authorities and fire authorities who are responsible for giving advice on safety matters. Students of venue fire safety at entertainment venues should read 'They never came home – The Stardust Story', a chronological account of the Stardust Disco fire written by Fetherstone and McCullagh (2001).

Sadly there appears to have been a reluctance to learn from the experience of others when it comes to fire safety. For example, in his research into risk, Brian Toft (1990) provided an example of how a fire at the Iroquois Theatre, Chicago, 1903, and a fire at the Coconut Grove Nightclub, Boston 1942 occurred in remarkably similar circumstances. Toft reveals that in both cases the decorative fabric of the interiors was highly flammable, exits were locked or had not been provided, both venues were overcrowded and neither establishment had trained staff to deal with emergencies such as fire. It would appear that all of these issues were relevant factors in the Stardust Disco fire.

In 2007 the government took the decision to adopt a completely new approach to guidance for fire safety. Rather than have one guidance document it was decide to publish eleven separate guides specific to one type of venue or situation. This was done to assist venue operators to conduct a mandatory fire risk assessment. The new guides refer to:

- Offices & shops
- Factories & warehouses
- Sleeping accommodation
- Residential care premises
- Educational premises
- Small & medium places of assembly
- Large places of assembly
- Theatres, cinemas & similar premises
- Open air events and venues
- Health care premises
- Transport premises & facilities

As each publication has its own distinctive front cover colour, fire guides are no longer referred to as the Yellow Guide. Further information on availability and use of the new guides can be obtained at www.opsi. gov.uk

The Event Safety Guide

The Event Safety Guide has also evolved from the seventies. Unlike other guides however the Event Safety Guide has undergone several name changes. The first guidance published to improve safety at concert events was the G.L.C. Code of Practice for Pop Concerts (a guide to safety health and welfare at one-day events) published in 1976. Commonly referred to as 'The Pop Code', the document was only intended for use in London but many local authorities throughout the UK quickly adopted the guide as a point of reference.

The Pop Code was published following a fatal accident at a David Cassidy concert in 1974. Cassidy was at the height of his popularity in 1974, he was a major star in a current TV show (The Partridge Family) and his records were worldwide hits. In his book published under the title, 'C'mon (sic) Get Happy', Cassidy (1994) revealed that for his 1974 tour advance ticket sales indicted that he would draw crowds of 30,000 to 40,000 people at sell-out stadium shows.

Personal security arrangements for the singer were given a high priority due to a reported attempt to kidnap the star the previous year. In 1973 the Los Angles Police Department (LAPD) had warned Cassidy that they believed a serious kidnap threat existed. Apparently the LAPD informed Cassidy that they had information to indicate that two known criminals planned to kidnap him and demand a ransom of $1m from his TV production company.

Fears for the singer's personal safety consequently led to a specialist security team to be formed for his world tour. Artistes Security Services Ltd provided the security team. While the prime purpose of a security team was to prevent a kidnap and ransom attempt there was also an important secondary role, namely that of protecting the singer from the often irresponsible actions of over enthusiastic fans that followed him in their thousands. Tight security therefore surrounded the singer at all times. The kidnap attempt never materialised. Whether this was due to an overt security presence or some other reason it is not known.

The penultimate concert of the 1974 tour was played at the White City

Stadium, London. Following this show Cassidy would play Manchester as the final date. The demand for tickets to see the performer at White City before the end of the tour was therefore very heavy. As a member of the Artistes Security Services team I witnessed a tremendous amount of crowd excitement and crowd surges were taking place constantly. In 1974 however we had scant knowledge of crowd surge phenomena and our focus of attention was on the safety of Cassidy himself.

At the end of Cassidy's White City concert the security team was aware that St. John Ambulance service had dealt with a great many distressed young people who had been extracted from the crowd by the front of stage pit team. We subsequently learned that 500 young women who had fainted or become over excited had been treated by first aid. Of this number 30 people had been taken to hospital for further treatment. There was nothing unusual in this; it had happened every night at every show around the world. Normally these casualties would be detained for only a few hours in order to calm them down and then be collected by relatives or sent home. On this occasion Bernadette Whelan, a 14-year-old schoolgirl was one of those 30 casualties who were taken to hospital for further treatment. Her condition was considered by medical teams to be far more serious than the other young women who had been brought in. Bernadette did not return home, she remained in a coma for four days before dying (Upton, 1995).

At the time there were confusing reports of the cause of Bernadette Whelan's death. Cassidy was informed that Bernadette had a history of poor health due to a heart condition and believed at the time that she had died as the result of a heart attack. In fact Dr Rufus Compton, the pathologist gave the cause of death at an inquest, as *"death caused by traumatic asphyxia. Obstruction of respiration was mainly a result of compression of the body. Her brain had been damaged by cardiac arrest"*. (Cassidy b). In layman's terms, she had been crushed to death.

In his book Cassidy quotes the Hammersmith coroner Dr John Burton who testified at the inquest as saying that, *"10,000 young fans had been crowded up against a barrier in the centre of the front of the stage, with no means of escape"*. The coroner went on to play a tape recording made at the concert where fans were clearly heard pleading to be taken out of the crowd crush.

Public outcry over the death of Bernadette Whelan continued long after

Cassidy's tour was forgotten. The Greater London Council (GLC) that governed London at that time set up an inquiry to look into the incident. The inquiry team's findings were the catalyst for the Code of Practice for Pop Concerts

It is generally accepted that the Guide to Health Safety and Welfare at Pop Concerts and Similar Events, published in 1993 replaced the GLC Pop Code as it was a national document rather than one intended for London. Once again end users overcame the Home Office passion for long titles by simply referring to it as the Purple Guide, a reference to the distinctive colour of the front cover. Like most other official guidance documents the catalyst for this one was a serious incident involving loss of life. The particular incident for this review of pop concert guidance was the Donington Monsters of Rock Concert of 1988, which resulted in the deaths of two young rock music fans. This accident has already been the subject of a case study in a previous chapter therefore there is no need to expand on it further in this chapter. Suffice to say that it served the entertainment industry well until 1992 when the Health and Safety Executive responded to a request from practitioners to upgrade guidance. The result was the publication of The Event Safety Guide, still referred to by practitioners as the 'purple guide'.

Legislation

Considerable legislation has been introduced for sports events and the use of stadia. People interested in these particular issues should read 'Sport and Safety Management' by Frosdick and Wally (1997). The book provides both a practitioner and a legal perspective on the introduction of legislation in the form of:

- The Safety at Sports Grounds Act 1975
- Sporting Events (Control of Alcohol) Act 1985
- The Fire Safety and Safety of Places of Sport Act 1986
- Football Spectators Act 1989

Those persons who are interested in the wider implications of legislation for the concert industry should look on the web for the work of entertainment lawyer Ben Challis who provides a comprehensive review in, 'Legal Aspects of Health and Safety at Live Music Events'.

Ben reviews a wide range of legislation that includes: criminal and civil law, Negligence, The Occupiers Liability Act 1957, The Criminal Justice and Public Order Act 1994, Event Licensing and Misuse of drugs. The Health and Safety at Work Act is also reviewed in terms of how it relates to live music events. Arguably the most important piece of legislation to emerge that directly affects the leisure security industry is the Private Security Industries Act 2001. The wide ranging implications of this Act are discussed in Chapter Ten.

Many issues, such as the law regarding searching of persons, powers of arrest, the use of force, misuse of drugs and human rights are mandatory subjects in current training courses. An assumption is therefore made here that persons entering the industry will undertake training at some level. Consequently these subjects will be covered in a training programme and there is little point in discussing them here. This chapter then focuses on specific legislation that has a direct impact on the crowd safety practitioner at concert events.

Public Entertainment Licensing

In a paper published by entertainment law specialist Popplestone Allen in 1993 it was explained that responsibility for public safety at regulated entertainment events is with the holder of a Public Entertainment Licence (PEL), granted by a local authority i.e. a County Council, London Borough or Metropolitan Borough. The granting of a PEL to an event organiser by the local authority generally covers the staging of a musical entertainment event. A PEL is intended to protect the safety of performers and the public attending any site or venue and is mandatory for any event where public dancing or music is the principle activity.

Permanent venues, such as a theme park or a stately home would normally be licensed on an annual basis. This type of PEL is renewed annually on payment of an appropriate fee subject to there being no alterations having taken place within the venue. Organisers wishing to stage a 'one off' event where no annual PEL is in place, may apply for an Occasional PEL. This is an obvious title for a licence application to use a venue or site only occasionally for public entertainment. The applicant(s) requesting an Occasional PEL are required to submit full details of their intended event, details of the venue, plus a curriculum vitae of themselves and key personnel associated with the venture. Of particular interest to the local authority would be the company or individual responsible for crowd management planning.

Initially the local authority will have to be satisfied that both the site and the event are suitable for the granting of a licence. Currently, suitability is judged on advice offered by a Safety Advisory Group (SAG). Normally SAG would be comprised of local authority technical staff, the Fire Service, the police and the ambulance service. Local residents are invited via the local press or public meetings, to express any objections they may have to the disruption that may be caused to the local community.

The person to whom a PEL is issued can be the concert promoter or the venue operator. Normally a PEL would stipulate conditions set for crowd capacity, crowd density level, ticketing arrangements, noise levels, car parking arrangements and catering and sanitary arrangements, all of which are mandatory conditions. The person to whom a PEL is issued cannot absolve him/herself from overall responsibility for public safety but they can delegate the task of crowd management planning.

Public entertainment licensing law applies to relevant events held throughout England and Wales. In Scotland, local authorities have powers to grant an entertainment licence for events such as pop concerts only when an admission charge is made. Graham (1993) revealed that the powers of English and Welsh district councils are in the Local Government (Miscellaneous Provisions) Act 1982. London boroughs have separate powers under the London Government Act 1963. Powers of Scottish district and island councils are contained in the Licensing Act (Scotland) 1976 and the Civic Government (Scotland) Act 1982. Licence conditions are usually set and enforced by local government Environmental Health officers, as is the relevant health and safety legislation. Where an event takes place on local authority owned ground the licence requirements are self-policed. In this situation the local authority is both promoter and licensing authority. Where such circumstances prevail, health and safety legislation is enforced by the Health and Safety Executive (HSE).

Once a licence is granted the venue and event is liable to inspection by a number of enforcement officers. These officers include the local authority licensing officer, emergency services, health and safety officers, food and hygiene and customs and excise officers. Normally enforcing officers would only enter a venue during the course of their duties to examine or investigate. John Shaughnessy (1993), Principal Licensing Officer for the London Borough of Brent has explained that, where a PEL is granted, the venue or event is subject to inspection by local authority inspectors who hold statutory warrants and are empowered to enter licensed entertainment premises at reasonable times to ensure that all is well. It is a criminal offence to obstruct them. As such all security staff must be aware that it is a criminal offence to obstruct an enforcement officer

Security Industry Act 2001

The introduction of the Private Security Industry Act (2001) created the Security Industry Authority (SIA) as the regulator for all the sectors of the Private Security Industry. The stated aim of the SIA is to raise standards of professionalism and skills within the private security industry. As such, the function of the SIA is to ensure that all staff supplied by a security contractor and individuals offering to provide a security service have attended appropriate training and hold a current license issued by the SIA. It is a criminal offence for a venue operator or company to employ an unlicensed security person. Directly employed security staff, i.e. a security guard employed in-house is exempt from licensing on the grounds that their background record is checked and the employer will provide training. At the time of writing however there is an ongoing debate over the role of the event safety steward. Some local authorities argue that all event stewards should hold a current door supervisor's license while the United Kingdom Crowd Management Association (UKCMA) and sport venues argue that stewards operate a customer care and safety role therefore door supervision training is inappropriate. Another area of discussion is that of the role of celebrity protection and/or VIP protection provided by foreign nationals visiting the UK with a client. As their stay in this country is often short term it is difficult to establish their exact status. Individuals often adopt a title of Personal Assistant (PA) etc for the duration of their stay, therefore the SIA appears to be reluctant to engage in what might simply be a time wasting exercise. Further information on security licensing can be found on the SIA web site www.the-sia.org.uk.

8 RISK ASSESSMENT

We have seen from the two previous chapters that the leisure security industry has had to learn some very hard lessons. We have also seen that a number of guidance documents are now available in the UK to aid the crowd safety practitioner to comply with legislation. Each of these documents emphasises the point that every employer has a mandatory obligation to carry out a risk assessment for their work activity. The term 'risk' however is open to any number of interpretations, crossing the road can present a risk if you look the wrong way before stepping off of the kerb. This chapter continues the theme of legislation to consider how the leisure security industry has had to come to terms with risk assessment in order to comply with the Health and Safety at Work Act.

In 1974 the Government in the U.K. introduced legislation in the form of the Health and Safety at Work Act. The Act made it mandatory for all employers to conduct a risk assessment for their work activity. The government appears to have assumed that all employers were capable of carrying out the task. Naturally there are some risks that are obvious, such as wearing protective clothing or ear defenders on building sites but, when your work activity involves the safety management of crowds, risk assessment can be a complex operation. It should be remembered that concert promoters who evolved from the fifties and sixties, and the leisure security industry that served them, did not undertake any form of training. Both groups were entrepreneurs earning a living simply doing something they enjoyed.

It is also a fact that, at the time that health and safety legislation was introduced, crowd safety management was not recognised as a social science. Consequently no nationally recognised qualification indicating the level of competence of a self-styled crowd manager was available until 2004 when Buckinghamshire Chilterns University College introduced the Crowd Safety Management Foundation Degree (FD). In their published research into concert crowd safety, Chris Kemp, Iain Hill and Mick Upton (2004) emphasised the point that prior to 2004 operational planning for crowd safety (including risk assessment) was largely a generic exercise based on the planner's previous experience.

It was my experience that many of the people who presented concerts in the seventies considered the Health and Safety at Work Act to be applicable only to factories, shops and offices. A popular opinion was that this new legislation had nothing to do with organising entertainment events. The full impact of the Act was perhaps not realised until as late as 1993. That year the Head of the Policy Branch of the Health and Safety Executive explained in an important seminar paper that a mandatory requirement for risk assessment was intended for *all* employers (Graham 1993). Naturally this includes event organisers and venue operators. In response to questions on how a risk assessment might be conducted, Graham explained that the basic principle of assessing risks were essentially to identify hazards and then evaluate the risks, i.e. the likelihood of the hazard arising and the harm it could cause. Furthermore, provided the assessment is carried out in a structured way, taking into account the known and foreseeable hazards, there should be no difficulty in identifying the significant risks and establishing the relative priority for action.

The realisation that a crowd manager might be held responsible for injuries caused to the public in a crowd related accident came as a shock to some people. Previously there was a widespread belief that crowd incidents were simply accidents or in extreme cases an 'Act of God'. It now appeared that a crowd manager might face possible arrest and prosecution in a case where negligence was indicated. The leisure security industry now found it necessary to introduce a comprehensive training programme for permanent management staff and a large number of essentially casual workers in order to comply with health and safety legislation.

A 1993 view that risk assessment was a straightforward exercise was somewhat optimistic however. It took another 12 years before structured training for risk assessment for crowd activity was introduced in the form of the first Foundation Degree (FD). The FD was introduced by Buckinghamshire Chilterns University College (BCUC) at the specific request of practitioners who expressed the wish to have more understanding of how to comply with health and safety legislation. A national training programme therefore evolved slowly, by taking into account the lessons learned from previous accidents and incidents, personal experiences and academic research into crowd activity.

Today a mandatory requirement to undertake a risk assessment for work activity is strongly enforced in the U.K. If your work activity involves crowd management or crowd control you are required to document how you intend to create a safe environment for the public and protect members of staff from hazards that might arise as a result of what is taking place. While the event promoter (or venue operator) is ultimately responsible for creating a safe environment, he or she can delegate responsibility where it is considered reasonable to do so. During the planning phase of a one-off major event the local authority will insist on documented evidence, in the form of a crowd safety management plan, before granting a Public Entertainment Licence (PEL). It follows that at permanent indoor venues risk issues form a part of the conditions of a PEL issued annually to that venue.

Risk Analysis

A logical first step in the risk assessment process is the risk analysis. At the ShowSec Training Centre I introduced what is known as the Extreme Value Analysis (EVA) approach to data gathering. EVA is perhaps best described as a system designed to learn from the past as the concept requires the researcher to consider previous crowd related accidents at a similar event in similar circumstances on two equally important levels, referred to as:

- *Low frequency – high intensity*
- *High frequency – low intensity*

A low frequency – high intensity incident is one that is rare but results in a high casualty rate. For example, a disaster that claimed the lives of 11 rock music fans attempting to get into the Riverfront Arena, Cincinnati, to see a concert by The Who in 1979 was essentially a failure of queue management. This incident clearly signals a need to understand queue theory. The overall aim of queue theory is to control crowd density prior to ingress. The theory is based on five considerations of planning:

1. Pedestrian approach to a queue system
2. Standing space within a queue
3. Unrestricted forward movement
4. Passing through an ingress system
5. Dispersal within the venue

While queue theory appears to be simple, and the leisure security industry has largely taken it on board, it would appear that others have not. In recent years there have been at least two 'near miss' incidents at retail outlets due to a lack of understanding of queue theory. At an IKEA store in Edmonton North London an estimated 6,000 desperate people caused chaos trying to get into the store in 2005 to purchase goods in a sale. Although this incident was widely reported by the media, the lesson was not learned as 3,000 people were involved in a desperate struggle to get into a sale at a Primark store in Oxford Street in 2007. In both cases a team of uniformed security guards failed to keep control and apparently police were called to restore public order.

The secret of success in terms of queue management is strict control of crowd density. I always based my calculations for queue management on the research carried out by the highly respected pedestrian planner John J. Fruin. Fruin's research argued that while standing in a queue is generally considered to be a static activity, body sway and foot-shifting are required to aid in the return of blood to the brain and the resting of leg muscles. My own research conducted on queue observations supported Fruin and further indicated that such body movements easily triggered spontaneous lateral crowd surge activity in bulk queue conditions. The simple answer therefore is to create linear queue lanes controlled by barrier systems managed by trained staff.

It was a combination of the EVA system with a discovery of academic theories that the leisure security industry had never previously been aware of and personal observations that allowed the industry to gradually introduce a range of training programmes to consider risk analysis.

A high frequency – low intensity incident can be any form of near miss situation such as pop/rock concerts where there might be high excitement and very high-density levels and people are extracted over the front of stage barrier for safety reasons. Usually there are few injuries but, as we saw in the last chapter, crowd pressure loads can be fatal.

The origins of a sterile zone concept, or pit, in front of a concert stage can be traced to the actions of sixties youth culture. The sixties decade brought about a change in rock 'n' roll style by introducing 'Beat Groups', typified by the Beatles and the Rolling Stones. Beat music introduced a change in cultural behaviour from dancing to spectator hero worship. The wish to touch, or hug, a 'pop star' became an uncontrollable urge for many young fans and accessible dance hall stages only served to encourage fans to invade the stage, often resulting in shows ending in chaos.

Initially orchestra pits were seen as a natural front of stage barrier due to the fact that they were often very deep and this in itself was considered at the time to be enough to deter stage invasions. Deep pits however soon presented an unacceptable hazard when determined fans attempted to climb over them and fell into the pit! Promoters overcame this problem by placing security staff in a line in front of the pit to act as an added deterrent but this only led to confrontation between security staff and the public. By the end of the seventies it was generally accepted that security teams should be stationed within a pre-fabricated pit barrier for two reasons: first to protect the stage and performers, second to assist persons in distress within the crowd.

Pit Teams

It was possibly a fatal incident at a Rolling Stones concert in America that altered the leisure security industry to the need for specific training for the team that man a pit. On December 6th 1969, the Stones played a massive free concert at a disused racetrack at Altamont U.S.A. It was at this concert that 18-year-old Stones fan Hunter Meredith was stabbed to death by Hells Angels who had been hired as front of stage security. At the time of the incident the Angels claimed that they acted to prevent an attempt by Meredith to kill Mick Jagger. It would appear that Meredith was armed with a handgun but witness accounts of the incident claimed that he (Meredith) drew the firearm only after he had been stabbed and beaten by the Angels and at that point he was in fact attempting to run away to escape his attackers. It was also alleged that once Meredith drew the weapon the Angels attacked him a second time. In the UK the lesson of Altamont was taken on board by Artiste Security Services who introduced a disciplined approach to pit teamwork.

Contemporary concert audiences are very active in terms of creating a powerful energy release. In this respect modern youth cultural activity is very different from that of previous generations and predicting the energy released by cultural behaviour and natural laws of dynamics are an undeveloped science. Spontaneous surge activity and cultural behaviour can result in literally hundreds of people being extracted from the crowd for their own safety. These high frequency low intensity situations dictate that specific training was needed for the teams that man a pit. Subsequently BCUC introduced a certificate in pit training. The one-day course was designed by trainers drawn from the membership of the United Kingdom Crowd Management Association (UKCMA) and the course now forms a part of standard training for staff at most of the major crowd management companies.

The risks associated with fire and crowd crushing during pedestrian flow was discussed in Chapter 2. The design of contemporary venues has greatly improved fire safety but the issue of crowd surge activity and subsequent crushing injuries remain today as a serious problem at some events. Natural laws of crowd dynamics dictate that peaceful crowd gatherings can build up tremendous pressure loads if the crowd is not effectively managed and controlled. In a crowd collapse or high-density situation the maximum response time should be three minutes if serious injury to victims is to be avoided. Beyond that time-frame the brain might be starved of oxygen. There is no fixed point at which human beings die when subjected to an intolerable pressure load, therefore it is difficult to identify the limits of human endurance to pressure. A British Home Office Report (1973) cited two fatal cases:

a) Death of one male was estimated to have taken place when subjected to an estimated load of 1400lbs (over 6kN) for 15 seconds

b) A man died when subjected to an estimated load of 260lbs (1.1kN) for 4.5mins

From these two cases it can be estimated that both high pressure for a short duration and medium pressure for a sustained period can both lead to death by asphyxiation. Prior knowledge of possible extreme behaviour would naturally require very careful crowd management planning if accidents are to be avoided.

Risk Documentation

At the time of writing the most popular approach to conducting a risk assessment is the so-called likelihood x consequences model. The Health and Safety Executive (HSE) published *Research Report No 53/1993*, which provided a formula for risk assessment in 1993 (Au *et al* 1993). The report recommended that a numerical figure could be applied to both the likelihood and the consequences of an accident. Explained further as follows:

The likelihood of an accident is rated as follows:

1	2	3	4	5
Very Unlikely	Unlikely	Possible	Likely	Very likely

The severity rating might be:

1	2	4	8	16
Minor bruising	Appreciable persons injured	Major multiple injuries	Severe hospital cases	Catastrophic fatalities

Where an accident is considered to be likely (4) and the severity rate was estimated to be severe (8) the risk factor for that particular activity would be 32 (8 x 4). In order to convert the risk factor to a risk level the report provides a risk category or band, for example:

1 - 16 = Low risk

17 - 31 = Medium risk

32 - 64 = High risk

65 - 80 = Very High risk

Using this system a risk factor of 32 would therefore indicate that this particular activity is high risk and management action is necessary to eliminate, reduce or manage that particular risk. It must be remembered however that when conducting a risk assessment for crowd activity the process must be repeated for *every* activity i.e. arrival, ingress, attendance, egress and final departure. The assessor cannot simply apply one risk factor fits all to the whole event.

On face value the numerical system appears to be perfectly logical but it should be remembered that awarding a number to either the likelihood or severity might simply be the personal opinion of the assessor rather than a scientific system of measurement. Another assessor might have a different opinion and therefore award a different number to the same activity; an assessor may in fact introduce any form of numbering system they chose as there is no mandatory requirement to use the HSE suggested system.

Where individual assessors can, and often do, introduce their own versions of numerical system, great care needs to be taken in order to avoid confusion. In a scenario where the assessor and the local authority officer (the recipient) are using different interpretations of a numerical system it is not difficult to imagine that the recipient might misinterpret the risk level that he/she has been given. Confusion can be avoided of course if the assessor submits his/her risk assessment methodology as a part of the risk documentation.

In fairness to the researchers who published the HSE numerical system it should be noted that Zachary Au appears to have later changed his mind. Au was a researcher for the 1993 report and he later published a second report under the title *Prototype Methodology for the Assessment of Risk to Crowds in Public Venues* (Au 1997) in which he criticised the numerical systems model and favoured an alphabetical system.

Criticism of a numerical system of risk assessment was in fact made one year before Au published his second report when Brian Toft (1996) published a critique of the limits mathematical modelling of disasters. Toft made a very important point when he argued that individuals create their own sets of criteria against which risk is interpreted. Toft was emphasising the fact that risk perceived by a given society or individuals are not objective but subjective. In other words, individuals perceive risk differently; consequently some people enjoy so called dangerous sports while others regard them as high-risk actions bound to lead to serious injury or even death. This is not to imply that the participant in a high-risk sport is irresponsible, rather that they feel that they are in control and are therefore managing risk.

Statement of Intent

A Statement of Intent (SOI) underpins the process of risk assessment. An SOI is not a legal contract but it would demonstrate to a court the level of responsibility accepted by a company during the period of provision of its services to a client. It is therefore of the utmost importance that a SOI is an unambiguous statement of the crowd managers understanding of an agreement. It naturally follows that the SOI is approved by the company insurers.

It is important to remember however that senior staff should never step outside of the terms of the SOI by offering casual advice to the client. For example, where a SOI indicates that a security company accepts responsibility for crowd control they are agreeing to implement a plan designed by others. The conditions of provision of a large number of contract stewards to a football match are that they would be working under the direction of the club Safety Officer. Their employer has no input into the design of the stadium or regulations that might be introduced. In such conditions contract staff should not offer advice or attempt to change any system in place since, as in the event of an accident a court might regard their actions as offering a professional service. A definition of a professional service assumes that *good advice* is being offered even when no fee is involved. Should this advice then prove to be wrong, the manager could be held responsible.

9
"LEAVE YOUR JACKET BEHIND"

This chapter reviews the role of celebrity protection in terms of how it emerged as a specialised industry in the sixties and evolved to become a major part of the leisure security industry today. The somewhat strange title for the chapter is taken from a casual remark made by my long-term friend Peter (Bear) Gauchi. Peter and I meet up regularly for endless cups of coffee over which we attempted to put the world right. During one such meeting we were discussing the effect on a celebrity bodyguard's (BG) life, when they return from the often heady atmosphere of a world tour, during which they travelled in private jets and stayed at five star hotels with the rich and famous. Returning to the real world where the most important immediate task is to take the wife shopping at the local supermarket or collect the kids from school does require some adjustment.

The Bear summed up the necessary reality check nicely when he casually remarked, *"when you finish a tour leave your tour jacket behind"*. Experienced tour personnel will know exactly what he meant by this remark. For the inexperienced, Peter was offering possibly the best advice ever on touring with the rich and/or famous. The tour jacket that Peter referred to is simply a metaphor for the false glamour of show business and when a person finishes a tour it is important to leave this false world behind. It is a mistake to believe that you have now become a good friend of the rich and famous. The BG is *not indispensable,* he/she is simply an employee. Your family and friends are the real world.

The role of the celebrity BG may appear to be glamorous and exciting to those who have only seen the Kevin Cosner movie 'The Bodyguard', but in reality it amounts to 14-hour seven day weeks of hard work. Travelling first class or in a private jet admittedly eliminates much of the tiresome tasks you can experience at airports but nevertheless, a need for constant vigilance and awareness is still very tiring, believe me.

This chapter, therefore, looks beyond the false glamour to trace the path that celebrity protection has taken over the years. My version of how this industry has evolved is based on my own personal experience, research conducted when I set up the ShowSec Training Centre and anecdotes kindly provided by highly experienced tour professionals who have become valued friends over the years.

In order to present a structured approach to the issues covered, I have split the chapter into sub headings, the first of which is that of attacks and assaults against celebrities. An attack can range from violent assault to murder; an assault can range from verbal abuse to violence. Attacks against the rich and famous in the sixties were the foundation stone of the celebrity protection industry and therefore this seems to me to be a logical place to start.

Next is the issue of kidnap, or possible kidnap attempts against a celebrity. Celebrity kidnap attempts have fortunately been few, but nevertheless, the possibility now forms a part of a modern day threat assessment. Following the discussion on kidnap, attention is turned to celebrity stalking. The stalking of celebrities first became an issue in the sixties and has now become a serious problem. This discussion considers lessons learned from the past and how the industry has had to adapt in order to learn how to recognise the signs of change from ardent fan worship to mentally unbalanced stalker.

The subject of armed response to threat is only considered here because there is a military school of opinion that argues that protecting celebrities should not be classified as the role of bodyguard. This argument is underpinned by the fact that the majority of celebrity protection people have, in the past, emerged from the private security industry and therefore have not undertaken long periods of firearm training to a level that highly trained specialist military and police teams have. This military view argues that as the celebrity BG is unlikely to have undertaken extensive firearm training they are not able to carry out the ultimate protection act, that of stopping an armed attack with deadly force. It is for this reason only that the issue of firearms is discussed.

Finally, the topic that I have labelled 'the unusual' considers the roles that celebrity BGs have found themselves involved in that are outside the norm for VIP protection. When a client requests a protection team it cannot automatically be assumed that it is an individual who is the focus of attention for the protection team. For example, in 1993 ShowSec International was contracted by the Times newspaper to provide a protection team for the World Chess Championship between current world champion Garry Kasparov and the UK challenger Nigel Short at the Savoy

Theatre, London. At the final briefing to discuss a threat assessment Team Leader Tony Ball discovered that it was not so much the personal security of the two players that was the prime concern. The primary reason for security was to protect information in the form of private discussions that each player might have with his support team in their hotel room. If important discussions were overheard game tactics might be revealed to the opposition. Consequently it was necessary to call in experts in electronic counter measures (de-bugging) and keep them on stand-by to constantly sweep each hotel suite. Once swept, strict access control was necessary throughout the period 7th to 30th October, the period of the championship. Tony therefore had to quickly change his focus of attention. Room security became the prime security function, escorting the players became a low threat secondary task.

Attacks and Assaults

The year 1966 might perhaps be considered to be the point at which a celebrity protection industry began to develop as a specialist industry in its own right. That year death threats were made against John Lennon during a Beatles tour of America and, as you might expect, security for the Beatles became a dual task of crowd control and protection. In a book charting the career of the Beatles, Philip Norman (1981) claimed that the Ku Klux Klan made death threats after Lennon had allegedly stated that the Beatles were more popular than Jesus Christ. In actual fact Lennon had been misquoted, he responded to a question by a newspaper reporter who asked him if Christianity or rock 'n' roll would vanish or shrink first. Lennon merely pointed out that bigger crowds now attended Beatles concerts than church. Lennon's innocent response to this question was picked up by the teenage magazine Datebook and misquoted to read that the Lennon regarded the Beatles to be more popular than Jesus Christ. What he intended was a simple statement of fact but in spite of his explanation, and an apology, the report caused widespread burning of Beatles records in the southern states of America. To the relief of Beatles fans around the world Lennon was only subjected to verbal abuse on the 1966 American tour.

A milestone in the creation of a the celebrity protection industry was arguably reached on the night of the 9th August 1969 (just three years after Lennon was threatened) when the heavily pregnant movie actress Sharon Tate and four of her friends were brutally attacked and murdered in her home in Los Angles. In his book, 'Sharon Tate and the Manson Murders', Greg King argues that *"her (Tate's) death on a hot summer night in 1969 changed attitudes in America for ever. It touched a raw nerve in a country shocked by the assassinations of John F. Kennedy, Martin Luther King, Robert F. Kennedy and Malcolm X"* (King 2000).

The shocking murder of Sharon Tate and her friends in 1969 did not just affect Hollywood. It also changed attitudes of celebrities and performers visiting America generally. British celebrities and performers intending to visit or work in America also remembered the threat to the Beatles three years earlier and they now demanded protection. It must be remembered, however, that protection services were not as widely advertised then as they are today. Managers with a responsibility for finding a BG had two possible avenues available by which they could find security staff:

1. Employ door supervisors working at clubs or venues frequented by celebrities

2. Contact a leisure security company

Both of these employment avenues were able to provide streetwise people with a tough reputation although it has to be said that these people were not trained professional BGs. On the plus side, however, this new breed of rock 'n' roll clients did not want a smartly dressed person who they often regarded as being an extension of the police service. What was needed was a jeans and tee shirt mentality that understood the full meaning of flexibility. It has been stated in an earlier chapter that Artiste Security Services Ltd were the UK market leaders in the provision of leisure security services in the sixties and the company was ideally placed to provide protection teams in the UK and abroad.

By the end of the sixties the provision of security staff to performing artistes on tour and in the home had become commonplace. Today security is still necessary for both. In 1995 a seriously deranged intruder was caught in Madonna's House in Los Angeles. I will return to this incident later in this chapter. Ex-Beatle George Harrison was attacked and seriously injured in his home at Henley-on-Thames, Oxfordshire, on the night of December 30th 1999 by Michael Abraham, 33, a mentally disturbed man from Liverpool. It was reported at the time that the police believed this was not a bungled burglary but a deliberate attack. Abraham was arrested on suspicion of attempted murder and detained in a mental hospital (BBC news 1999). Previously another alleged mentally disturbed person, Christin Kelehar, had been discovered on the 23rd December at Harrison's home in Hawaii. She was found sitting at a kitchen table eating and drinking. A police report of this incident alleged that Kelehar was dangerous and would have tried to attack Harrison had he been at the premises (Whelski 2000).

More recently, three masked men, reportedly armed with a knife and an iron bar, broke into the home of pop star turned TV celebrity Kerry Katona shortly before midnight on the 16th July 2007. In the Daily Mail, Liz Hull reported that two men held Katona and her five-month-old baby hostage while the third man forced her husband to take him around the house selecting valuable items to steal. After collecting an estimated £150,000 worth of jewellery and other items, the three men made off in the couples £65,000 BMW car. Press reports of the incident speculated that Katona had not switched on a sophisticated intruder alarm system installed at the house (Hull 2007).

Outside the home a verbal or physical attack on a celebrity can occur anywhere, sometimes without any warning. While literally thousands of people might idolise a famous person there is always the odd person that will take offence at their fame. An assault on a celebrity can come from a jealous boyfriend or husband, or a person who simply wants to impress their friends, usually when they have had too much to drink.

I have personally had to deal with a number of such incidents that ranged from verbal abuse to violent attack. On one occasion a man tried to attack the television presenter Mike Smith while he was live on air during a Saturday night live television programme called 'Noel Edmonds' Late Breakfast Show' on BBC1. I was working with Mike at an outside broadcast location in Newcastle. In the middle of a transmission, watched by millions of viewers, a man suddenly charged at him shouting and swearing. Now, when working on television programmes the golden rule is stay out of camera shot, so I was squatted down out of view approximately three metres from Mike. Fortunately I managed to get to my feet, reach the attacker and take him down about a metre in front of Mike while at the same time keeping him quiet. The Saturday night television audience never knew what was going on but I clearly remember the startled look on Mike Smith's face as he nervously spoke to the viewers. Mike finished the insert in true professional style. In the chaos that followed afterwards the guy ran off and I never did discover what he was so angry about.

The period when a performer is exposed on live television or performing on a stage is possibly the point at which security is most likely to be compromised. Stage invasions by over excited fans were once a standard part of a show and, to be fair, some performers actively encouraged such activities.

The need to prevent stage invasions in order to protect an artiste was first considered in the sixties when stage invasions at ballrooms with very low stages were common. In the majority of cases stage invasions were simply over excited fans who wanted to touch their heroes but an attack on a performer in the seventies indicated a more serious problem. On the night of December 10th 1971 the American group Mothers of Invention played a concert at the Rainbow Theatre, London. That night jealous boyfriend Trevor Howard (24) jumped onto the stage and pushed front man Frank Zappa off of the stage into the front of stage pit. Zappa was taken off with a broken arm and the show cancelled. It appears that Howard's girlfriend was a big fan of Zappa and although she had never had any form of contact with the performer he decided in a fit of rage to take drastic action.

As we saw in the last chapter, front of stage security is now taken very seriously at major concert events. The area known as the pit is now the subject of much debate in terms of design for safety and security. Improved front of stage safety pits have reduced the possibility of an attack on stage but it can still happen. Robbie Williams found this out when he was knocked off the stage into the pit at a concert at the Schleyerhalle Stadium, Stuttgart, Germany on the night of 21st February 2001. A 20-year-old-man in the audience apparently decided that the person on stage was not the real Robbie Williams but a clone. He managed to get onto the stage and push the singer off into the pit. Fortunately Williams was not seriously harmed on this occasion and he continued with the show. The attacker was held by security staff and handed over to the police.

The need to conduct on-going risk and threat assessments is standard practice for the BG in order to take into account how the level of risk or threat can suddenly change dramatically. For example, in a newspaper article for the Daily Mail, Anderson (2006) records that in 1967 the Jewish singer/actress Barbara Streisand made a movie called Funny Girl in which she co-stared with the Egyptian actor Omar Sharif. This was at a time when Israel was at war with her Arab neighbours and the pairing of a Jew and an Arab caused a great deal of ill feeling. Streisand reportedly received death threats, which immediately caused an upgrade in security from her normal level for a concert tour to possible deadly attack. The conflict in the Middle East has change little since 1967 and the same situation could easily occur today.

Kidnap

Incidents of kidnap and ransom involving celebrities are surprisingly low. This is perhaps due to the fact that a successful kidnap requires the kidnapper(s) to conduct an extensive surveillance operation to carry out a kidnap. Celebrity movements on a tour of appearances, or while playing for a team, are high profile, but tours normally only involve a short duration stay in any one city. The local promoter or event organisers will be responsible for security arrangements and, in addition to BG teams, celebrities are likely to be surrounded by local security and/or police. At home the level of protection will be lower and very sophisticated domestic intruder alarm systems incorporating CCTV are now available and avoiding routine can reduce travel risk.

It would be foolish however for a celebrity BG to ignore the potential for kidnap regardless of how remote the threat may appear. Lessons have been learned from high profile kidnap incidents that stretch back over the years. On 8th December 1963 Frank Sinatra's 19-year-old son Frank Jr. was kidnapped as he left a venue in America unprotected. Reports of the incident claim that Frank Sinatra paid $240,000 to secure his son's release. Three people were eventually arrested for carrying out the kidnap. The actor singer David Cassidy has also written about an attempt to kidnap him at the height of his fame in his book *C'mon Get Happy*. As stated in an earlier chapter, Cassidy employed a regular security team from Artiste Security Services Ltd.

In 2002 BBC News reported that Scotland Yard had foiled an alleged attempt by an eastern European gang to kidnap Victoria Beckham, wife of England football captain David Beckham. Previously the police had foiled an attempt to kidnap Victoria Beckham and her son in January 2002. Another football player to attract the attention of a kidnap gang is Thierry Henry. A Sunday newspaper reported that an imminent threat to kidnap the player's two-year-old daughter had caused him to employ 24-hour security (Gladdis K & Whiteside P 2007).

During my time as Chairman of ShowSec International there were a number of occasions when our teams employed anti-kidnap drills because we suspected that there might be an attempt to snatch a performer who we were tasked to protect. As none of our clients were ever kidnapped it's not possible to know if we foiled any attempts or not. The only time that we had any possible indication of a possible kidnap attempt was during a tour of Italy by a well-known UK pop group. The Bear was the artistes BG and as they left a venue after a concert their local driver stopped when a car suddenly pulled across the front of them. The driver jumped out of the car and ran off. Bear quickly dived across into the driving seat, re-locked the doors, drove across the centre reservation and sped off in the opposite direction. A report of the incident was made but the Italian police decided that the driver ran off in panic from what they (the police) felt was a near miss vehicle accident and no action was taken.

The provision of protection for top class celebrities and sports personalities has now moved away from the exclusive realm of the door supervisor to take a position more in line with corporate protection. This is due largely to the introduction of mandatory security licensing in the U.K. which has brought in standard training programmes that cover issues such as threat assessment and counter surveillance measures. The impact of security licensing on celebrity protection is discussed further in the next chapter.

Celebrity Stalking

No discussion on celebrity protection would be complete without reference to stalking. Very few of us who work in the industry have not encountered stalkers at some time. During my time at ShowSec International the company dealt with 34 cases of alleged stalking activity. Confidentiality agreements prevent me from naming the victims, but at this point I have to admit that not all these cases proved to be genuine. A few were imaginary, some were fabricated by publicity agents who at one time appeared to believe that a person was not truly a celebrity until they had a stalker. There were others however that required high-level security cover. In one case an internationally famous female singer was even stalked by a man who was in prison. He regularly wrote what can only be described as inappropriate letters to her and when she did not respond he then made threats to kill her on his release. Fortunately he is still in prison but the victim still dreads the thought that one day he might be released and come looking for her.

Arguably it was the murder of John Lennon that brought celebrity stalking to prominence in a BGs approach to risk assessment. On the 8th December 1980 mentally deranged Beatles fan Mark Chapman fired five shots from a .38calibre handgun at Lennon as he entered his New York apartment building. Four shots hit him and one missed. Chapman waited calmly at the scene until police arrived to arrest him.

The problem of stalking (celebrity or otherwise) should be recognised as a serious criminal offence. Initially it was regarded as nuisance, or simply the price of fame. The police largely ignored non-celebrities who suffered the trauma of stalking and some people would argue that this is still the case today in the UK.

When I set up the ShowSec Training Centre little was known about celebrity stalking but it was obvious that it should be an important subject on our VIP protection training courses. To begin with much of the material used on our courses to illustrate the problem was drawn from the experiences of our own members of staff working on the celebrity protection circuit. Later I discovered a book entitled *Stalkers – Harmless Devotion Turns to Sinister Obsession* - written by Jean Ritchie (1994). I drew heavily on Ritchie's excellent study of stalking to develop our training programme. I would still regard her book as having great value today for those people that have an interest in celebrity protection.

One of the first lessons I learned about dealing with stalkers was that it is important to get a balanced view in order to establish a threat level. To do this I categorised potential stalking activity as, *intrusion, harassment* and *malicious stalking*. Intrusion obviously has many levels that can range from interrupting a meal in a restaurant for an autograph to looking through a window of their house in an attempt to take a photograph. Most celebrities are willing to chat and sign autographs but there are times when it is not possible, such as when you are rushing to catch a plane or train. In this scenario the BG is expected to play the bad guy by pulling the celebrity away while they protest that they would much rather stay and chat. The celebrity BG therefore has to plan for a number of possible scenarios to cope with persistent requests for an autograph or to take a picture. In a discussion on intrusion with the actor David Soul, he explained to me that, *the worst scenario is visiting a public toilet, because just as you stand at the trough someone will approach you and ask for an autograph!*

There are some individuals who get their kicks from insulting celebrities.

On one occasion I was eating a meal at a motorway service station with the singer actor David Essex when a man approached our table and asked for an autograph for his girlfriend. David immediately stopped eating produced one of his publicity photographs and asked for the girlfriend's name. He then signed the photo and handed it over. The man accepted the photo and as he turned to walk away he said, *"she thinks you're great but I think you are crap"!* Now David Essex happens to be one of the easiest people to work for and he is known as a person who will always take time to chat to people. The guy's remark was totally uncalled for; it was total ignorance and simply designed to impress the friends he was with. David just shrugged his shoulders and told me to ignore it. The writer David Gritten (2002) recounts a similar situation in his book *Fame.* Gritten explains how a man, claiming to be an ardent fan, approached the actor Steve Martin for an autograph while he was having lunch in a Los Angeles restaurant. On this occasion Martin apparently held up his hand simply as a gesture to indicate that he was eating and did not wish to be disturbed. As the disgruntled fan turned away he apparently said, *"well screw you",* then turning to people on the next table he said *"a big shot".*

Fans that have queued all night for concert tickets and dash out to buy the new record release obviously deserve to be treated with respect but, at the same time, asking them to wait until you have finished a meal is hardly the attitude of a big-headed star. Knowing when a dedicated fan steps over the line to become an obsessive fan however is an important personality shift that the celebrity BG must learn to quickly recognise.

A worrying trend in the intrusion scenario now is the modern day use of technology to track celebrities. The idea started in America with the emergence of www.gawker.com in New York. The site invites people to text in if they spot a celebrity in Manhattan. The spotter is requested to take a photograph with their mobile phone, if possible, or text information such as who the celebrity is with, what they are wearing, what they are doing and their exact location. Information provided is then put up on a map on the web site for others to descend on the area to spot the celebrity. The site claims to have hundreds of people logging on each day. A disturbing feature of this seemingly harmless tracking of celebrities is that the paparazzi now have hundreds of people out on the streets unknowingly spotting for them.

The paparazzi are not always the evil people that they are made out to be however. It must be remembered that when the celebrity was on the bottom rung of the fame ladder they may have desperately courted the paparazzi. For as the journalist Peter Mckay (2006) has noted, *"there is a class of celebrity who thrive on paparazzi pictures, being famous is their one occupation"*. Once they have achieved fame however they only wish to be photographed on their terms. This can in turn upset photographers who feel that they have the right to unrestricted access to the celebrity.

A whole new celebrity magazine culture now exists to cater for those people who wish to become famous for doing very little and those that want to read about them. This culture has in turn created a new source of income for the celebrity BG. Magazines now regularly employ security teams at celebrity weddings in order to ensure that they get exclusive photo rights. Some magazines will pay a new breed of paparazzi large sums of money for what are termed *'interesting shots'* of celebrities at social functions. An interesting shot is a photograph of a person caught unaware, typically with a funny facial expression. But some paparazzi will deliberately try to take a picture up a woman's skirt in the hope that she is not wearing underwear! In this scenario we are looking at unacceptable behaviour or harassment.

Harassment is defined by the Collins English Dictionary to be, *"to trouble, torment or confuse by continual persistent attacks or questions"*. The late Diana Princess of Wales is often cited as a person subjected to continual harassment, and some might argue that it was paparazzo harassment that was the root cause of the accident in which she died. Photographers on the other hand might claim that it was public interest that compelled them to follow her everywhere and that Diana often encouraged media attention. While there are always two sides to any argument it is difficult to understand the constant attention that the paparazzi gave to Prince William's girlfriend Kate Middleton on occasions when she was simply getting into her car to go to work. The actions of the photographer pack on those occasions were clearly harassment in my opinion but nevertheless not classified as *malicious* stalking.

J.R. Melor, Professor of Psychology at the University of California, has explained malicious stalking to be:

Repeated unwanted contact by any means that might lead to a credible threat to a victim. Includes: making threats to a victims family or friends, publication of offensive material on the internet, sending offensive material through the post, public statements, offensive acts involving the victims possessions or property. (Melroy J.R. 2000)

Professor Meloy's detailed study of stalking goes on to classify it as follows:

- Simple obsessional: individuals who have had a previous relationship with the victim. Stalker seeks revenge or to control the victim.

- Love obsessional: development of a fanatical love for the victim but there is no real relationship. Total love of the victim by the stalker.

- Erotomaniacs: have no real relationship but firmly believe that the victim is in love with them. Delusion

My experience has been that Professor Melroy got it spot on with his classification system and it is the basis to undertaking a threat assessment for a very complex problem. Dealing with a stalker is an extremely difficult task that takes a good deal of tact and understanding. The temptation to get tough with them should be resisted and you cannot reason with them. It is nevertheless an issue that the celebrity BG often has to deal with today. The private security industry has now advanced to a point where there are companies and consultants that specialize in the provision of a counter stalking service.

Armed Response

I thought long and hard about covering the issue of armed response. I finally decided it was necessary to touch on the issue because of the view of some military trained BGs, mentioned at the beginning of this chapter, that a person cannot operate in a close protection environment unless they are armed. Not all security professionals share the view that firearms play a vital part in protection. In his book, 'Close Protection The Softer Skills', ex Royalty Protection officer, Geoffrey Padgham (2006), makes the point that: *"history has shown that statistically the reality is that during an attack on a protected person, they* (firearms*) are very rarely used as a means of defence"*. As this observation is made by a person who spent 27 years of his police service working at the highest level of close protection, it must be respected. Padgham did not imply that BGs should not be armed; obviously there are situations where it is necessary. His point is rather that the case for carrying weapons is often overstated. It is also important to remember that the carrying of any form of weapon is illegal in many countries.

It is a fact however that many BGs currently operating on the celebrity circuit are ex-military and therefore have benefited from extensive firearm training. Possibly the most publicised example of an ex-military person using a firearm to protect a celebrity is that of American celebrity protection specialist Basil 'Steve' Stephens. In 1995 Steve was tasked to protect Madonna and his responsibilities included overseeing security at her residence in Los Angeles. At approximately 1900hrs on the evening of the 29th May 1995 an intruder triggered an alarm as he climbed over the wall of the property.

Steve focused the residence CCTV system on the area and immediately recognised the intruder as a mentally unbalanced person who was stalking Madonna in the firm belief that she was his wife and that this was his house. Steve immediately called the police and, assisted by another security person, went to intercept the intruder before he could enter the house. In the confrontation that followed the intruder appeared to attempt to draw a weapon while making threats to kill Steve Stephens who then moved to draw his own weapon but stopped when he realised that the intruder had not produced a weapon. At this point Steve attempted to calm the intruder by speaking to him and the second BG went to the front gate to admit the police. Suddenly angered by the fact that Steve was preventing him from what he regarded as his own house, the intruder lunged at Steve and attempted to take his weapon from its holster. In the struggle that followed Steve drew his firearm and shot the intruder in the leg. The Los Angeles Police report of the incident considered Steve's action to be a measured response and no action was taken against him as a result of the incident.

This incident is not quoted in support of carrying a firearm, rather as an example of an incident where a licensed firearm was used defensively by BG. Threats and attacks of this kind are something that all BGs on the celebrity circuit must be prepared to assess and manage. This does not imply that firearms are necessary, rather that armed support *might be* required in some circumstances. Needless to say the BG who is not firearm trained and fully licensed should *never* carry one.

The second example is that of an unarmed BG who was prepared to deal with a person who was believed to be armed. This example is less dramatic but nevertheless required a high level of professionalism. My old friend Dave Moulder was on a tour of America with rock star Ozzy Osbourne when, just before the show was about to start, venue security staff reported to him that a man in the audience appeared to have a gun concealed under his jacket. Fearing that this person might attempt to attack Ozzy, Dave knew that he needed to remove the source of the threat from the audience. Dave is a highly trained ex-military weapons specialist able to quickly identify many types of firearm but he needed a reason to get close to the suspect without causing alarm or panic in the audience. He went into the audience and quietly spoke to the person in question, telling him that he was selecting fans to meet Ozzy before the show. The intention being to take him somewhere quiet and disarm him. Dave reasoned that if the guy intended to harm Ozzy he would jump at the chance to get close to him. The man immediately agreed to follow Dave out of the audience but suddenly became suspicious and ran off before he could be retained and searched. The police were called but he escaped. Who knows what might have happened if Dave Moulder had not been on hand to deal with the situation.

During my own career I was asked on two separate occasions to carry out a maintenance check on a handgun. The first time was when an Arab Prince asked me to clean a new Browning 9mm that he had just bought. The second occasion was some years later when a European concert promoter asked me to strip down and clean a Colt 45 that he had legally purchased. As there was no imminent threat to either of these individuals and I was not required to carry a firearm on either of these assignments I can only assume that it was my reputation that was being tested. Presumably, if I had failed either of these two tests I would have been dismissed.

The debate on firearms obviously does not include those Close Protection Operatives (CPOs) working in the so-called hot spots such as Iraq and Afghanistan. The private security operations in these areas are carried out primarily by what are termed Private Military Contractors (PMCs), a reference to the fact that the majority of the people undertaking such work are ex-military personnel. A condition of employment for this role is to be fully competent with firearms.

In his book 'The Modern Bodyguard', the highly experienced and respected CPO and Close Protection trainer Peter Consterdine (2006), draws attention to the fact that there is now what he calls a blurring of distinction between the work of PMCs and commercial close protection. Peter provides an interesting contrast between the role of PMC operations in Iraq and the movement of a Principal in the commercial world. He rightly points out that a PMC movement from A to B in Iraq is basically a military convoy whereas in the commercial CP world planning a night out in downtown Moscow will be a much more covert operation. Peter goes on to argue that it often comes as a shock to PMCs to find that on returning to the UK from Baghdad they find that they are still required to undertake 150 hours of training in order to obtain a UK operator's licence.

Peter Consterdine operates internationally for high-level corporate clients therefore prior to embarking on a protection detail in Moscow (or anywhere else), he would have carried out a very intensive intelligence gathering operation in order to establish a realistic threat assessment. An intelligence gathering operation is often a lengthy exercise and Peter would have involved numerous high level contacts that he has cultivated over many years in each area of his visit. In addition, he will have established reliable support (armed if necessary) in each area. This is not the sort of thing that a new CPO, ex-military or otherwise, can just suddenly do. For those who are interested in a full range of training in VIP protection, the books published by Peter Consterdine, Geoff Padgham and Jim Brown are all recommended reading by BCUC.

The Unusual

The last section of this chapter looks at some of the more unusual tasks that celebrity BGs have had to deal with or become involved in. For example, you are not always required to protect a person, it can be an item of clothing. I was once called in by the BBC to work on an episode of the television programme Eastenders where I was tasked by programme producer Julia Smith to protect a wedding dress. The scenario was that two leading characters in the show were to be married as a part of a story line and the Radio Times magazine had exclusive rights to publish a photo of the bride in her wedding gown. Naturally this meant that no other photographers were allowed to take pictures. The wedding scene was shot at a church in hospital grounds in Hertfordshire and somehow this was common knowledge among the paparazzi who turned up in droves. If they had got shots of the gown it would have killed the Radio Times exclusive deal stone dead.

The dress was actually brought in by the wardrobe mistress who simply strolled in with it in a bag. Once the actress involved got changed, however, she needed to move about the set and it became very difficult to keep the paparazzi from getting their shots. I managed it by blocking off camera vantage points with large BBC vehicles and asking the electricians to set up stage lights which pointed out toward the photographers at strategic points. Just as the bride was about to walk down the aisle the electricians switched on blinding lights directly toward the paparazzi making it impossible for them to take a picture.

Protecting integrity rights has now become a common feature of celebrity protection; most fashionable weddings today have photo deals with magazines and security teams are needed to prevent the paparazzi getting pictures. The paps will get up to all sorts of tricks to get their shots however. When Madonna married Guy Ritchie in Scotland BG Paul Dalanegra called in Mark Hamilton's team from Rock Steady Security to secure the church and Mark found one pap hidden inside a giant church organ. It appeared that he had been hiding in there since the day before!

Even when you are tasked to protect a person, however, it is not always a straightforward detail. For example, in 1966 I was employed to protect the world heavyweight boxing champion Muhammad Ali when he arrived in the UK to fight our champion Henry Cooper at Highbury Stadium. You would imagine that nobody would be foolish enough to take a swing at the champion of the world and you would be right. My task was to stop people attempting to shake hands with him. He was so popular that everyone wanted to shake his hand and, if they all had done so, it was possible that his hands might have been bruised – which could have affected his punching power in a world title fight. When you consider that an important feature of many musicians is their hands you can see how the BG needs to adjust their approach to protecting an artiste.

There are also rare occasions when a BG is employed with instructions to make sure that the VIP does not know that they are being protected because the VIP does not like security. In 1983 I was again employed by the BBC, this time to protect Ken Livingstone when he being interviewed at an outside TV broadcast at the London Zoo. Livingstone is apparently an animal lover, hence the location. The circumstances surrounding this detail were that Livingstone, as leader of the Greater London Council, had previously invited Sinn Fein leaders Gerry Adams and Danny Morrison to London for talks on the situation in Northern Ireland. Livingstone was a strong supporter of Irish republicanism and this made him a target for loyalists and the last thing that the BBC wanted was to have him attacked on live television. A team was therefore made to look like members of the production crew so that we could follow him throughout his stay. He must have wondered why these guys with clipboards seemed to follow him everywhere and we all sighed with relief when he left.

A celebrity BG has to learn to come to terms with a number of issues that are not taught on training programs. In November 1999 Rob Koslowski was detailed by ShowSec to protect a famous movie actor who was on an 'unofficial' visit to the UK. The actor was Superman star Christopher Reeves and his unofficial visit meant a private meeting with an insurance company. Christopher Reeves had been involved in a horrific accident, which had left him paralysed five years previously. With his principal confined to a wheelchair and needing constant medical attention it was obvious from the start of this detail that Rob was going to be involved in far more than threat assessment - welfare became the key factor.

Rob had to arrange for an ambulance and paramedics to meet the actor's private plane without the normal international arrival procedure. This was achieved by having the plane taxi into a hanger where it was meet by immigration. From there he was taken by ambulance to his hotel.

Prior to the arrival Rob had checked out the hotel. Normal procedures for a celebrity entering a hotel i.e. alternative routes etc were not practical. It was necessary for the actor to be transported in a service lift that was big enough to hold the Principal in a wheelchair, his staff, medial team and life support equipment. This required careful measurement of lifts, corridors and doors en route. In the room a specially designed bed designed for people with spinal injuries was provided and extra power supplies, transformers and a generator installed in case of power failure. Oxygen was also provided as back up. Not the normal sort of checks made by a Security Advance Party (SAP) but, as Rob put it to me, *"every single job is different on the celebrity circuit. You don't know what the next job will involve, we are always facing a different challenge."*

Sadly celebrity BG teams also get tasked to protect funerals. During my time in the industry the most distressing was the funeral of the six-year-old son of Led Zepplin singer Robert Plant in May 1977. On this occasion team member Ron Franklin found a paparazzi hiding in the bushes at the church waiting to get a picture of the small coffin. It was difficult to ask him politely to leave. The same year I was a member of the team that protected the funeral of Marc Bolan, which was attended by David Bowie and Rod Stewart. In September 1980 I was a member of the security team at Zeppelin drummer John Bonham funeral. John was only 32 years old and I had worked with him many times. The most memorable funeral that I worked on was that of Diana Princess of Wales in September 1997. It was anticipated that huge crowds would assemble along the route from the day before and this proved to be the case. ShowSec were asked to provide 800 stewards to man points along the route to allow police officers to focus on security issues. This sad occasion marked a turning point in the relationship between private security and the Metropolitan Police. Previously the police had refused to allow private security teams to operate on public streets but from 1997 on they have been allowed to and private security companies now regularly carry out crowd control operations on London streets.

Perhaps one of the most important lessons that people who choose celebrity protection as a career have to learn is that there are occasions when it is OK to laugh at yourself. I learned this lesson early on when comedian and satirist Barry Humphries approached me to provide a close protection team for a press conference for a show he was putting on at the Theatre Royal Drury Lane, in London. The conference was intended to promote a show by two famous characters created by Humphries, Dame Edna Everage and Sir Les Patterson. Humphries wanted a team of big guys dressed in suites and wearing dark glasses to portray a completely over the top security situation. On the day I rigged up security detector arches that each reporter had to pass through and of course we controlled the alarm system. The first reporter to come through was David Wigg from the Daily Express who was a little irritated by the fact that he constantly triggered the alarm and I kept asking him to remove items of clothing. I first asked him to remove his jacket but by the time I asked him to take off his shoes and socks he realised that he was being set up and he immediately joined in the fun. When Dame Edna appeared 'she' explained that her security team loved her and were prepared to protect *'her'* against any unwarranted press intrusion. Consequently, every time a question was asked from the floor two huge BGs would position themselves shoulder to shoulder directly in front of the person that raised the question. It turned out to be great fun for all involved and of course Humphries got maximum publicity for his show.

On another occasion a situation that was not intended as a joke caused uproar due to the failure by an American production manager to understand

British military uniform dress. I was working with the American singer/ actress Dolly Parton at the time and she was booked to record a television show at the Dominion Theatre in London. The producer had seen the state opening of parliament and he decided that a military guard of honour for Dolly would look great on screen. He asked me if I could find some troops to take part and I told him that I could arrange for the Household Cavalry to do it but they were not allowed to wear their ceremonial uniforms for such events. The problem was solved by the production manager agreeing to hire the correct uniforms from a theatrical costume supplier. He assured me that he had seen the uniform on TV and knew exactly what was needed and I booked 20 soldiers to take part. When I arrived at the theatre I was told that the military were refusing to take part and what's more they were looking to kill me! On meeting up with them I discovered that the production manger had hired Yeoman Warder costumes, as worn at the Tower of London, and the uniform included red tights. The idea that 6' 4" guardsmen should wear tights did not amuse them. I eventually managed to talk them into it but it cost the production manager several cases of beer.

I also had to get a BG team to overcome their embarrassment on another occasion when I was asked by TV presenter Noel Edmonds to provide a protection team at an event at Doncaster Racecourse for the character Mr. Blobby created by Noel for his show Noel's House Party. The character arrived by helicopter to be met by his security team with a golf cart. He then undertook a tour of the site presidential style with his security team escorting on foot. At first it was difficult to find four BGs willing to do the job as they felt it demeaned the role of the BG. Eventually I convinced people to take part because it was an event aimed at young children and most of the guys who agreed to take part had families. The reaction from the literally thousands of youngsters lining the route made the whole thing worthwhile and at the end all the team wanted a photograph taken with Mr. Blobby.

My final unusual story involved two old friends of mine, Dave Moulder and Ron Franklin, who worked with Wham in the eighties. In 1985 they were both members of the tour party for the Wham tour of China. When the tour moved on from Peking the backing band, management team and two security flew on to Canton while the two stars remained in Peking for interviews. For the security team to travel separately from the principal(s) might sound unusual but it is quite common on the celebrity protection circuit.

During the flight Dave Moulder was seated next to the Portuguese trumpet player Raul de Oliviera. Forty minutes into the flight Dave noticed that Raul appeared to behaving erratically. Thinking that it might be flying that had caused the problem Dave spoke to him to calm him down. At this point, however, Raul produced a Swiss Army knife from his hand luggage and threatened Dave. Ron Franklin realised that something was wrong and he cam forward to assist and at that point Raul suddenly stabbed himself in the stomach. Other passengers fled to the rear of the plane and band manager Jazz Summers went to the cockpit to warn the pilot. The pilot thought it was all a part of a highjack plot and he quickly put the plane into a steep dive and returned to Peking. Dave and Ron managed to render first aid to the injured Raul until they had landed and he was rushed off to hospital.

The sequel to this story was that the Chinese medical team then insisted that Dave stay on watch at the hospital until Raul was well enough to leave while Ron rejoined the tour. Consequently Dave found himself looking after the trumpet player rather than the two principals.

The SAP

We cannot leave a discussion on celebrity protection without mention of the important role of the security advance party/person (SAP), or as they are often referred to on concert tours the 'venue security person'. Following the tragic death of a young woman in a crowd related incident at a David Cassidy concert in 1974 it dawned on me that an SAP was necessary at major concert events for two reasons. Firstly (and most important) to ensure maximum standards of safety for the public that attend the event and secondly to protect the reputation of the performer(s). A visit to a concert event is supposed to be fun; no performer wants newspaper headlines of serious accident and injuries.

The problem in 1974 was that very few of us understood the complex issues involved with crowd safety planning, therefore it took the industry years to fully appreciate how important the SAP role was. The concept of a tour SAP was adopted from a military/police system but it required a more flexible approach than that of military teams who are taught that the SAP supervises the arrival and departure of the VIP. The celebrity often flits from one country to another during a tour to check out venues. Therefore clients, and their accountants, were reluctant to pay for a person on a tour who they did not see a value in. After all, it was the responsibility of the local promoter to provide security and make sure everything was safe. In fairness it has to be said that, even when clients were convinced of the need, many people who took on the role of an SAP took it for granted that their role was confined to backstage security issues only.

One of the first people to realise the importance of crowd safety to the reputation of a performer was American tour security person Bob Wein. I first met Bob in the eighties when he toured the UK with artistes such as Bruce Springsteen. He quickly impressed me as being a person who fully understood the importance of the SAP role. He constantly questioned the pedestrian flow systems and arrangements to control density that we had put into place for his artiste and he was fully in tune with what we were trying to do at the ShowSec training centre. As the years went by Bob became a good friend as he took on the role of the tour SAP more and more and today many of the world's most famous acts rely on him to ensure maximum safety standards at their shows.

Today a tour SAP is normally only employed for a major tour by an internationally famous artiste and a good one operates on three levels. On one level their role is similar to that of a corporate protection SAP, that is to say they are responsible for ensuring proper security systems are in place for local travel, accommodation and at the venue in each city and country due to be visited. On another level they would check that conditions specified in a performer's tour contract rider have been adhered to. Rider conditions can include suitable hotel accommodation, dressing room facilities and arrangements made for transportation by the local promoter. The most important role the SAP has is that of event or venue crowd safety examiner. This requires the SAP to have a working knowledge of crowd behaviour, dynamics and pedestrian flow systems for ingress and egress.

10 2007

What we now refer to as the leisure security industry has flourished and grown for over 2000 years. In the UK this growth has taken place within a diverse range of activities and venues and, until the year 2001, it was totally unregulated. Although licensing improved the image of the industry it failed to take the diverse nature of leisure security into account. This was due in a large extent to a reluctance by the Security Industry Licensing Authority (SIA) to consult with key industry organisations such as the United Kingdom Crowd Management Association (UKCMA) who repeatedly tried to negotiate with the SIA, but all attempts failed. Consequently the SIA failed to understand the important differences that exist between crowd management, crowd control and security. The full impact of this lack of understanding was perhaps not realised until as late as 2006 when an attempt to licence football stewards was strongly resisted by the clubs on the grounds that stewards were employed in the role of customer care – they were not security. This argument had in fact been put forward for discussion by the UKCMA to the SIA some years before but had been completely ignored.

In the wake of crowd disasters at football matches several measures had been introduced to improve crowd safety. These measures included the concept of a Safety Advisory Group (SAG), Safety Certificates, the creation of the role of a club Safety Officer and all-seated Premiership grounds. In addition, the Football Licensing Authority (FLA) introduced training for stewards in the form of the Certificate in Matchday and Event Stewarding (CEMS) and the Football Safety Officers Association (FSOA) has also introduced training for their role that is in line with National Vocational Standards (NVQ). These initiatives were introduced independently – however, football authorities did not see it necessary to negotiate with the UKCMA either, which is strange considering that the membership of the association provide staff to many football clubs.

Football provides only a minority share of income to most major leisure security companies. The bulk of their income comes from casual green-field site events or contracts held with stadiums, arenas, theatres and clubs that stage several events per week. The UKCMA strongly support national standards of training but felt that the extremely high fees charged to them for a CEMS steward training programme was far too high. In addition CEMS courses appeared to take far too long to deliver. The UKCMA therefore took the option of using the programmes introduced by other training bodies that were far cheaper and could be delivered within a few days. As these programmes sat at Level 2 on the National Occupational Standards (NOS) the football authorities were compelled to accept them at sports grounds.

For candidates to gain an award at Level 2 on the NOS they must undertake training with a trainer approved by a recognised awarding body. At base level the NOS Level 2 steward qualification can be taken with trainers approved to instruct CEMS, City and Guilds, NVQ or NCFE. The acronym NCFE is used rather than an organisation name. Event stewards do not need a security license. Door supervisors are also at Level 2 on the NOS but they are classified as security, therefore they do require a security issued by the SIA to work. It is a criminal offence for a contract door supervisor to work without a licence and approved trainers must include specific core elements, as specified by the SIA, in their courses.

While the issue of training for stewards and door supervisors had been addressed by UKCMA membership, the question of management training and qualification remained. The Safety Officer course introduced by the FSOA was considered to be too narrow an approach to crowd safety management. Safety officers operate in an architecturally designed environment, therefore they do not need to calculate density or design pedestrian flow systems. Their primary role is to ensure that existing systems that were designed by an architect and approved by a SAG team remain functional and safe. It is a far different story at a rock concert at a green-field site where a crowd manager has to calculate systems to cope with crowds of 100,000 plus people who will attend an event for 12/14 hours. During this period the crowd will be exposed to weather and the antics of performers that often encourage extreme forms of behaviour.

For management training the UKCMA membership chose to get involved in the Buckinghamshire Chilterns University College (BCUC) Foundation Degree (FD) programme. The FD was introduced by the UK Government in 2001 to encourage wider participation in education, improve skills in employees, and provide an opportunity for staff to gain a qualification whilst in the workplace. The current BCUC FD courses are two years distance learning with regular two-day workshops. On graduating with an FD a person can go on to take a one year top-up to gain BA (Hons) and on to a Masters course if they wish.

Where other academic institutions focused their crowd studies mainly on the underlying social causes of public disorder, Professor Chris Kemp at BCUC quickly realised that the introduction of the new Foundation Degree (FD) was the way forward to establishing a qualification for the management of peaceful crowd activity. This was exactly what the leisure industry was seeking and I was pleased to work with Chris in the design and implementation of what became a very successful course.

My input into the crowd safety management FD course was based on a traditionalist view of crowds. Arguably the widest read of traditional theorists is Gustave LeBon. LeBon's (1895) Psychological Law of the Mental Unity of Crowds thesis argued that there can be a radical transformation of the individual into a primitive, irrational state of a mass of people, characterised by loss of self control, anonymity of the individual, primitive behaviour, suggestibility and a collective mind. LeBon identified three influences as being primary causes of a crowd single mind state:

Anonymity, a state, which could cause individuals to abandon responsibility for their actions,

Contagion, a phenomenon of a hypnotic order in which crowd actions is contagious,

Conditioning, a state of fascination where an individual that is immersed in crowd action soon finds himself in the hands of the hypnotiser.

LeBon's theory has been criticised by contemporary theorists due to the fact that it was written at a time of Paris street riots and therefore only relevant to public disorder. Crowds at rock and pop concerts, however, do appear at times to act with a single mind. It appeared therefore that LeBon had a place in modern crowd management planning. A very interesting contemporary concept was found in the *sites and strangers syndrome* established by Barry Turner (1997). Turner's syndrome drew attention to the fact that the use of sites and locations for purposes different from the intentions of the design, and the presence of people, who are not familiar with the site, create conditions that require specific analysis of risk. Once again this theory argument seemed ideally suited to a concert event held at a green-field site. For data regarding the design of pedestrian flow systems I called heavily on the published research of John Fruin (1993), Brian

Toft's (1990) thesis 'A Failure of Hindsight' and his work on risk analysis (Toft 1996) and the work of Toft and Reynolds (1978) on organisational learning. All combined to form a dual traditionalist and contemporary theoretical approach to the training programmes I designed. Support for theoretical concepts was obtained by field studies conducted at concert events across Europe by students at BCUC. Field studies were organised by Chris Kemp and supervised by Iain Hill. Concert promoters and the Mojo barrier company also provided valuable support by allowing us unrestricted access to their events.

An important feature of the crowd safety management FD program is the development of a command and control system when planning a crowd management operation. A command and control concept was introduced by the Metropolitan Police in London following serious public disorder at the Broadwater Farm housing estate in Tottenham, North London. The system is now widely used by the emergency services. The concept operates on three levels, Strategic, Tactical and Operational. The Cabinet Office (2002) provides a definition of the concept as follows:

> **'Command'** is defined as "the authority for an agency to direct the actions of its own resources (both personnel and equipment)"
>
> **'Control'** is defined as "the authority to direct strategic and tactical operations in order to complete an assigned function and includes the ability to direct the activities of other agencies engaged in the completion of a function". The control of the assignment functions also carries with it responsibility for the health and safety of those involved.

The emergency services operate a command and control system on three levels, **'Operational'**, **'Tactical'** and **'Strategic'**. These are more commonly referred to as **'Bronze'**, **'Silver'** and **'Gold'** respectively. The three levels cannot transpose across exactly from the emergency services to the leisure security industry but the system can work well generally. In a police system Operational Commanders will typically be located at the event and the security industry equivalent is the Team or Area Supervisor. A police Tactical Commander will typically be located close to the event, for example the Police Match Commander (or Silver Commander) at football matches. At a casual concert event the leisure security industry equivalent would be the Crowd Manager or Head of Security. A police Strategic Command will typically be located away from the scene, for example at Police headquarters or a venue dedicated for such purpose.

At strategic level (Gold) operational planning and the commitment of resources by a leisure security company is the role of a senior management officer who is likely to revert to the role of crowd manager/head of security (a tactical role) at the actual event. A social event therefore has no separate strategic command in terms of the crowd management organisation. If a serious incident occurred the police would take over a site and coordinate a major incident response by the emergency services.

More recently sector skills councils have introduced Level 3 (Supervisor) and Level 4 (manager) qualifications. In 2007 BCUC introduced Foundation Degree Protective Person for those persons that held an SIA CP licence and a BA (Hons) and masters degree, making it possible for a person to join the leisure security industry at any one of three levels levels and progress to Masters level. The model below illustrates how this can be achieved.

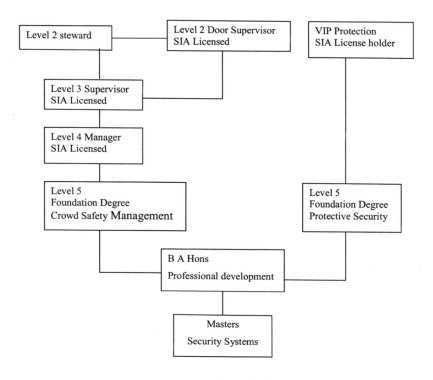

It can be seen from the above model that the safety steward does not need a licence as their job description defines their role to be that of customer care. Most leisure security companies, however, require their staff to obtain an SIA licence if they wish to progress. Companies see the door supervisor licence to be more appropriate than a static guard licence. All contract security staff are required by law to hold a current licence.

To obtain an SIA close protection licence it is necessary to complete a mandatory 150-hour training course with a trainer approved by an Awarding Body. Personnel serving with the military or police who have completed a specialist CP course and have a minimum of 50 hours CP operational experience do not require an SIA licence to register for a Foundation Degree. They would however require a licence if they acted as a civilian contract BG.

I think that it would be fair to say that leisure security has not always enjoyed a good relationship with the police and some might argue that this is still the case. A lack of trust has been due largely to the fact that police contact with the industry over the years has been largely based on their experience dealing with allegations of criminal acts by door supervisors and car wheel clampers. It is generally accepted that it was the actions of door supervisors and wheel clampers that was the catalyst for the introduction of legislation to licence the private security industry.

The relationship between the police and leisure security has improved greatly in recent years however. There have been two possible reasons for this improvement. On the one hand more police forces have come into contact with leisure security at major concert events and been pleasantly surprised by the degree of professionalism and knowledge of the practitioners. One example is a statement made in a seminar presentation to the Home Office Emergency Planning following the two Oasis concerts at Knebworth in 1994. In his presentation, Superintendent Paul Dumpleton of the Hertfordshire Police stated that the police service should accept that the leisure security industry has more expertise than the police when it comes to the management of peaceful crowds.

In the same year Paul Dumpleton made this statement Sergeants Malcolm Ding and Ian Ellison from Essex Police Public Order Training contacted me. Essex Police had been concerned over crowd activity at a recent outdoor concert by the pop band 'Take That' at which there had been a barrier collapse at the front of stage. The police service trains extensively for crowd control in public disorder situations and the energy expelled by a pop crowd was something of a mystery to them.

Following on from our meeting a series of training courses on crowd safety planning at concert events was organised. The feedback from the first course was that all officers would benefit from this training. The course went on to run for five years with officers attending from a number of county forces but unfortunately closed due to budget cutbacks. Since its closure, however, police officers have signed up at BCUC for FD programmes. The first serving police officer to gain a FD was Sergeant Jill McCracken, who is a member of the Hertfordshire Police planning team. Police officer graduates from the second FD course were Superintendent Jed Stopher and Sergeant Chris White from Essex and Sergeant Tony Wright from the Metropolitan Police and the 2007 induction course includes officers from South Wales. Apart from the police service other graduates from the BCUC FD programme include Geoff Long, Emergency Planning officer London Ambulance Service, management officers from the NEC Arena, practitioners from major leisure security companies in the UK and Northern Ireland and Australia and future courses are heavily booked.

REFERENCES

Chapter 1

Brightwell, J. 1996: Secrets of Lost Empires. The Colosseum *The Concrete Revolution p150*. BBC Books

Johnson, B. 2006: The Dream of Rome. Harper Collins

Taplin, O. 1995: in Oxford Illustrated History of Theatre: Ed John Russell Brown; *Part One: The First Theatres, Greek Theatre*. Oxford University Press

Wiles, D. 1995: Oxford Illustrated History of Theatre: Ed John Russell Brown: *Part One: The First Theatres, Theatre in Roman and Christian Europe*. Oxford University Press

Chapter 2

Bliven, B. 1944: *The Voice and the Kids p.10* in Faber Book of Pop ed Kureish H. & Savage J. Faber and Faber 1995

Booth, M. *et al* 1995: *Nineteenth Century Theatre p319* in Oxford Illustrated History of Theatre. Oxford University Press

Craine, D. 1956: *Rock Age Idol That's Elvis - Daily Mirror 30 April 1956* p45 in Faber Book of Pop ed Kureish and Savage. Faber & Faber

Daily Telegraph 1956: The Fifties: A Unique Chronicle of the Decade: *Rock and Roll, Cinemas Call Police p118*. Simon and Schuster Ltd. 1991

EPC: Data sheets issued by Emergency Planning College (now the Cabinet Office Planning College), Easingwold

Frith, S. 1978: Sound Effects: Youth, Leisure and the Politics of Rock 'n' Roll: *Rock and Mass Culture p47*. Random House Inc. USA

Kelly, K. 1998: *Sinatra the Man*: Daily Mail 19.5.98. p32.

Keepnews, O. & Grauer, B. 1960: *New Orleans Joys Chapter 1 p3*: in A Pictorial History of Jazz: People and Places from New Orleans to Modern Jazz. Hamlyn Publishing Group.

Kureish, H. & Savage, J.1995: *1942-56 'Grovey Fantastic Scenes' p5*: Faber Book of Pop. Faber and Faber

Lewis, P. 1978: The Fifties: *Youthquake p130.*: Book Club Associates

McElwaine, B 1955: *Is Johnnie Ray a Mass Hypnotist?* in The Faber Book of Pop p31: ed Kureishi & Savage. Faber and Faber 1995

Murrells, J. 1974: The Book of Golden Discs: *Million Selling Discs 1912 p10*. Barrie & Jenkins

Richard, K. 1987: Quoted on p58 in Part two Are The Kids All Right?: Ed Fuller G.J. Times Books

Robins, J. 1992: The Worlds Greatest Disasters: *The Iroquois Theatre 1903 p148*: Chancellor Press.

Tobler, J. Frame P.1980: *55 Rock Around the Clock*: p14 in 25 Years of Rock 'n' Roll. Hamlyn Publishing Group

Walker, D. 1992: *Carnegie Hall*: p23 in American Rock 'n' Roll Tour. Thunder Mouth Press

Chapter 3

Fuller, G. J. 1981: Are The Kids All Right?: *Part two p52*. Times Books

Lewis, P. 1978: The Fifties: *Youthquake p130.*: Book Club Associates

Walker, D. 1992: American Rock 'n' Roll Tour: Thunder Mouth Press

Chapter 4

Clayton, T. 1967: The Protectors: London: Oldbourne

Draper, H. 1978: Private Police p18 –20. Sussex: Harvester Press

Fruin, J. J. 1993: *Prevention of Crowd Disasters by Crowd Management, P104* in Engineering For Crowd Safety ed Smith R.A. & Dickie. Elsevier Science Publishers B.V.

Murfet, D.2004: Leave It To Me. Gardiner Books

Chapter 5

Ball, T. 2006: Unstructured interview with Tony Ball, Managing Director, Show & Event Security Ltd.

Grant, M. 2006: Director of Special Events Security Ltd: Unstructured interview.

Hamilton, M 2006: Recorded interview with Mark Hamilton, Founder and Chairman Rock Steady Security Ltd.

Strutt, P 2006: Recorded interview with Pat Strutt, Commercial Director, Olympus Security Ltd.

Wise, T 2006: Recorded interview with Terry Wise, Founder and former Chairman of Goldrange Security Ltd.

Chapter 6

Upton, M. 2004: Monsters of Rock Donington 1988: Course module paper for Crowd Safety Management FD course: Buckingham Chilterns University College

Upton, M. 2004: Disaster at the Atrock Festival: Course module paper for Crowd Safety Management FD course: Buckingham Chilterns University College

Chapter 7

Cassidy, D. 1994: C'Mon Get Happy: *Chapter 12, p134*: Time Warner

Elliot *et al* 1997: Table 2.1 p13, Disasters and Incidents Involving UK Stadia or Supporters: Chapter 2 The Failure of Legislation by Crisis: Sport and Safety Management Frosdick S & Wally L. Butterworth-Heineman

Challis, B. 2004: Legal Aspects of Health and Safety at Live Music Events: *Chapter 4*

Fetherstone, N. & McCullagh 2001: They Never Came Home – The Stardust Story. Marlin Publishing

Fire Prevention No 158: A review of the official report on the Stardust disco fire p 18. Fire Prevention.

Frosdick, S. & Wally, L 1997: Sport and Safety Management. Butterworth-Heineman

Graham, P. 1993: *Specific Legislation for Indoor and Outdoor Public Entertainments*: Published seminar paper, P220 in Engineering for Crowd Safety, Ed R.A. Smith & J.F. Dickie. Elsevier Science Publishers BV.

Robins, J: The World's Greatest Disasters: Football Tragedies 1964, 1971, 1986, p 106. Chancellor Press 1992

Smith, R 1992: Catastrophes and Disasters: *Disaster at Ibrox, 2 January 1971, Fans are crushed on a stairway, p186*. W & R Chambers

Poppleston, Alan 1993: *Public Entertainment Applications Licensing Procedures*: Seminar paper presented to: Health Safety and Welfare at Pop Concerts: Home Office Emergency Planning College, Easingwold, 15th December 1993.

Shaugnassey, J 1993: *Local Authority Procedures and Safety Inspection Strategy*: p10 in Focal Guide to Safety in Live Performances: ed Thompson, G. Focal Press

Toft, B. 1990: Thesis: The Failure of Hindsight: *1.3 Systems Failure and Cultural Readjustment Model, p4*. University of Exeter

Upton, M. 1995: *Principles of Good Crowd Stewarding*: *Death of Bernadette Whelan*: an unpublished seminar paper presented to Lessons from Crowd-Related Emergencies: Emergency Planning College, Easingwold, July 1995

Chapter 8

Au S.Y.Z. Ryan M.C. Carey M.S. Whalley S.P.: Managing Crowd Safety in Public Venues: HSE Contract Research Report No 53/1993: *Risk Prioritisation p5.16 – 5.18*. HSMO 1993

Au Z 1997: Prototype Methodology for the Assessment of Risk to Crowds in Public Venues. HMSO

Fruin, J.J. 1987: Pedestrian – Planning & Design. Elevator World Inc

Hopkins et al 1993: *Crowd Pressure Monitoring*: Published seminar paper in 'Engineering for Crowd Safety',ed Smith R.A. Dickie J.F. Fruin J.J. Elsevier. Science Publishers B.V.

Kemp, C., Hill, I., Upton, M. 2004: *A Comparative Study of Crowd Behaviour at Two Major Music Events*: Entertainment Technology Press

LeBon, G. 1895: *Crowd Unity of Mind Theory*: In The Crowd. Transaction Publishers 1999

Toft, B. 1996: in Accident and Design, ed Hood C. & Jones D.K.C.: *Limits to The Modelling of Disasters, p101 Implicit assumptions about risk.* UCL Press

Winsor, 2004: *Risk Assessment and the Identification of Hazards at Live Music Events*: Chapter 3 in Health and Safety Aspects in the Live Music Industry: ed Kemp C & Hill, I. Entertainment Technology Press

Chapter 9

Anderson, C. 2006: newspaper article The Prince and Funny Girl: P 50, Daily Mail 1st May 2006

BBC 1999: Television news report: *attack on George Harrison at his home deliberate*: 30th December 1999

Casidy, D. 1994: *C'mon Get Happy, Chapter 12:* Ed Chip Deffa. Warner Books Inc

Consterdine, P. 2006: The Modern Bodyguard: The Complete Manual of Close Protection. Protection Publications

Gallager, R. 2001: *I'll Be Watching You.* Virgin Publishing Ltd

Gladdis, K & Whiteside, P. 2007: News of the World report 29th July 2007

Gritten, D. 2002: *Fame – Stripping Celebrity Bare.* Allen Lane The Penguin Press

Hull, L. 2007: *Kerry and her baby held at knifepoint in £150,000 raid*: Newspaper Report p3 Daily Mail Tuesday 17th July 2007

McKay, P 2006: Quoted in Peter McKay Column P14 Daily Mail 27th May 2006

Melroy, J. R. 2000: *The Psychology of Stalking: Clinical and Forensic Perspective*: J.Reid. Academic Press

Norman, P. 1981: *Shout* – the true story of the Beatles. Hamish Hamilton Ltd

King, G. 2000: Sharon Tate and the Manson Murders: *Prologue P7*. Mainstream Publishing

Padgham, G. 2006: *Close Protection – The Softer Skills*: Introduction p 22. Entertainment Technology Press

Ritchie, J. 1994: *Stalkers – how harmless devotion turns to sinister obsession.* Harper Collins

Whelski, J. 2000: Feature article, *Harrison Back Home After Attack*: in Rolling Stone Magazine 3rd Jan 2000

Chapter 10

Berlonghi, E. B. 1993: Engineering for Crowd Safety, Ed R.A. Smith & J.F. Dickie: Understanding and Planning for Different Spectator Crowds: *2 Crowd Management versus Crowd Control p 14*. Elsevier Science Publishers B.V.

Cabinet Office 2002: *The Emergency Services Response to Disasters and Major Incidents*: Civil Contingencies Secretariat: Emergency Planning College, Easingwold: 31/08/00 ESResponse/RWoodham.

Canetti, E. 1992: Crowds and Power. Penguin Books

Fruin, J. J. 1993: in Engineering For Crowd Safety ed Smith R.A. & Dickie.

LeBon, G. 1895: *Psychologie des Foules*: Quoted in Crowd Psychology and Engineering: a paper presented to, Safety and Science seminar June 1994 by Dr. J. D. Sime, Published 1995.

Toft, B. 1990: Thesis: The Failure of Hindsight: *1.3 Systems Failure and Cultural Readjustment Model, p4.* University of Exeter.

Toft, B. 1996: in Accident and Design, ed Hood C. & Jones D.K.C.: *Limits to The Modelling of Disasters, p 101 Implicit assumptions about risk.* UCL Press.

Toft, B. Reynolds S. 1994: Learning from Disasters: *Organizational learning – helping change safety culture p8.* Butterworth-Heinemann Ltd.

Toft, B. & Reynolds, S.:1: Learning from Disasters: *Introduction 1.3 Safety Culture.*

Turner, B. 1978: *Sites and Strangers Syndrome*: in Man-Made Disasters. Wykeham Press

INDEX

Abba 53
Abbey Road Studios 52
Abraham, Michael 146
Acropolis 13
Aimcarve 102, 103
Ali, Mahummad 158
Altamonte 60
Anderson, Dave 49
Anderson, David 25
Aquilina, Frank 44
Arad 14, 101, 111-114, 118
Arden, Don 57
Artistes Car Services 57, 58
Artiste Services 53, 56, 60, 62, 67, 70-73,
    76, 78, 96
Artistes Security Services 56, 58, 60, 62,
    63, 72, 126, 127
Artistes Services 11, 56, 58-61, 70-79,
    82, 89
Astoria Theatres, Finsbury Park 56
Atrock Festival 111, 112
Ayres, Andy 65

Ball, Tony 77, 82, 88, 89, 94, 105, 107,
    108, 110, 145
Banister, Freddy 64
Barbican Centre 85, 86, 87
Basset, Fred 59, 71
Battersby, Simon 84
BBC 16, 31, 40, 78, 79, 107, 146, 147,
    149, 157, 158
Beatles 36, 47, 51, 52, 57, 59, 60, 145,
    146, 151
Bedford Theatre 27
Betesh, Danny 51
Big Brother 93
Billboard 28
Black, Don 57
Blackbushe 64
Blivin, Bruce 29
Bolan, Marc 159
Bonham, John 160

Booth, Michael 23
Boston Arena 32
Bouncers 24, 27, 31, 36, 37, 48
Bowie, David 159
Boxing Board of Control 50
Bradford City Football Club 87
Brightwell, Robin 16
Britpop 82
Broadwater Farm 168
Brooklyn Theatre, New York 24
Brown, Jim 157
Buckinghamshire Chilterns University
    College 12, 100, 133, 134, 166
Burton, Dr John 127

Cabinet Office Emergency Planning College
    (EPC) 26
Café Royal 45
Cairnlea Drive stair system 122
Caister Holiday Camp 69
Callaghan, Jim 59, 71
Callaghan, Paddy 59
Capital Radio 89
Capitol Cars 58
Cassidy, David 53, 62,126, 149, 162
Certificate in Matchday and Event
    Stewarding (CEMS) 165
Challis, Ben 128
Chandler, Alan 58, 67, 70, 71
Charlton Athletic Football Club 61, 87
Clarke, Raymond 99
Clayman, Barry 57
Cleveland Arena, Ohio 32
Cliff Richard and the Shadows 35
Close Protection Operatives (CPOs) 156
Close Protection – the Softer Skills 154
Coconut Grove nightclub 125
Cole, Henry 20
Coles, Richard 67
Collins, Patsy 59, 70
Colosseum 16, 18, 19, 20, 21
Compton, Dr Rufus 127

Concert Security, Birmingham   77
Consterdine, Peter   156
Cooper, Henry   50, 158
Corbishly, Jon   83, 99
Covent Garden Theatre   24
Cox, Des   50
Craine, Donald   34
Crockford, Paul   79
Crowd Management Centre   9
Crowd Safety Management Foundation
      Degree   133
Croy, Peter   76
Crystal Palace Football Club   89
Crystal Palace National Sports Centre   88
Cucchi, Fred   76

Daily Express   160
Daily Mail   29, 147, 148
Daily Mirror   27, 34
Daily Telegraph   33
Dalengra, Paul   158
Daltry, Roger   62
Diana, Princess of Wales   84, 153, 160
Dickens, Barry   57
Ding, Malcolm   99, 170
Dominion Theatre, London   33, 161
Doncaster Racecourse   161
Donington   64, 65, 81, 82, 93, 101-105,
      111, 118, 128
Door supervisors   24, 48, 49, 92, 131, 146,
      150, 166, 170
Dumpleton, Paul   170
Dunkly, Brenda   78
Eastenders   157
Edinburgh Playhouse   76
Elliot, Tony   80
Ellison, Ian   99, 170
Emergency Liason Team (ELT)   111
Empire Palace Theatre, Edinburgh   25
Endemol   93, 96
Epidaurus   14
Essex, David   53, 152,
Essex Police   99, 170
Evans, George   29
Everage, Dame Edna   160

Event Safety Guide   126, 128
Event Suppliers Association (TESA)   100

Fagan, Jim   44
Farr, Rickki   61
Ferguson, John   67, 69, 71
Fielding, Danny   59, 71
Fields, Sid   28
Finsbury Park Empire   28
Fire Safety and Safety of Places of Sport
      Act 1987   122
Football Association   88
Football Licensing Authority   165
Football Safety Officers Association   88,
      165
Forsythe, Don   44
Forum Cinema, Kentish Town   30
Foundation Degree in Crowd
      Management   9
Frame, Pete   34
Francis, Billy   59, 63
Francis, Danny   69
Franklin, John and Terry   69, 71
Franklin, Ron   67, 71, 80, 81, 159, 161, 162
Freed, Alan   31
Frith, Simon   30
Fruin, John J.   72, 135, 136, 167
Fury, Billy   35

Galbraith, Stuart   99
Genesis   66
Going Live   78
Goldrange   75, 85, 86, 87, 88, 97, 100
Goldsmith, Harvey   61, 64, 76, 81, 100
Gore, Wally   59, 71
Gough, Paul   96
Grand National   98
Grant, Mark   96, 99
Grant, Peter   57, 70
Greater London Council   111, 128
Greek Theatre   11, 13
Gritten, David   152
Guide to Fire Precautions in Existing Places
      of Entertainment and Like Premises
      123, 125

Guide to Health, Safety and Welfare at Pop
    Concerts and Similar Events   111,
    128
Guns 'n' Roses   103, 106, 108, 110

Haley, Bill   32, 33
Hamilton, Mark   76-78, 95, 99, 158
Harding, Mark   84, 95, 100
Harrison, George   146
Hatherall, Ben   63, 64, 65, 69, 71
Haymarket Theatre   24
Health and Safety Executive (HSE)   130
Hells Angels   53, 60, 137
Hippodrome   21
Holland Security Company   84
Holly, Buddy   47
Home Department   122
Home Office Emergency Planning
    College   99
Horch, Bert van   84
Household Cavalry   161
Howard, Johnny   49
Humphries, Barry   160
Hutchings, Dennis   96, 99
Hutton, Lyn   58, 66, 69, 71
Hyde Park   60, 84, 92

Ibrox   122, 123
IRA   44, 45
Iroquois Theatre, Chicago   24, 125
Israeli Concert Promoters Association
    (ICPA)   101, 112, 117

Jagger, Mick   53, 137
J J Security, Stafford   77
Johnson, Boris   22
Johnson, Steve   109
Jolson, Al   28
Jones, John   77
Jones, Maurice   103
Jones, Nigel   96

Katona, Kerry   147
Kay, Annette   58
Kemp, Professor Chris   10

Kennedy Street   76
Kerwin, Martin   79
King, Greg   146
King, Paul   80
Knebworth   63, 64, 65, 66, 67, 82, 92, 170
Koslowski, Rob   159
Kray, Charlie   64
Ku Klux Klan   145
Kureishi, Hanif   29

Lacamo   35
Langs Victoria Music Hall   26
Leavesden Film Studios   93
LeBon, Gustave   167
Led Zepplin   58, 159
Legends   69
Leisure Security Industry Conference   99
Lennon, John   145, 151
Lewis, Peter   33
Lewis, Vic   56, 57
Lictor   21, 22
Limb, Richard   111
Live Aid   81
Live and Kicking   78
Livingstone, Ken   158
Logan, Mark   84
London Borough of Brent   130
London Palladium   28, 34
London University   20
Long, Geoff   171
Los Angles Police Department
    (LAPD)   126
Loughborough Town Hall   111

MacDonald, Jim   76, 77, 95
Machina   115
Machinery and Transport Company   55
Madonna   146, 155, 158
Marshall Arts   76
Martin, Steve   152
Maxey, Bob   69, 71
Mayfair   35
McCartney, Paul   47, 52
McCraken, Sergeant Jill   171
McElwaine, Bernard   34

McKay, Peter 153
Melor, J. R. 153
Melroy J. R. 154
Meredith, Hunter 53, 60, 137
Merseyside Police 98
Metropolitan Police 84, 92, 160, 168, 171
Middleton, Kate 153
Millwall FC 87
Milton Keynes Bowl 9, 81
Mojo Barriers 168
Monsters of Rock 65, 81, 82, 93, 101, 102, 103, 128
Morris, Harry 44
Most, Micky 57
Mothers of Invention 148
Moulder, Dave 69, 71, 80, 155, 156, 161, 162
Murfet, Don 56-68, 71, 78, 82
Murfet, June 57, 58
Murrells Nook of Golden Discs 32
Music Hall 11, 23, 24, 26, 27

New Musical Express 28
Night Watch Services 55
Noel Edmunds' House Party 78
Noel Edmunds' Late, Late, Breakfast Show 147
North West Leicestershire District Council 111
Nottingham Castle 79
Numan, Gary 81
NYPD 30

Oh Boy 35
Olympic Games 13
Olympus Security 75, 92
Olympus Security Industry Authority 96
Only Fools and Horses 78
Osbourne, Ozzy 155
Osmond Brothers 53
Outlaw Agency 79, 80

Padgham, Geoffrey 154
Page, Jimmy 67
Paramount Theatre, New York 29

Parton, Dolly 161
Patterson, Sir Les 160
Peppermint Park 69
Personnel Plus 86
Pike, Paul 64
Pit teams 137
Plant, Robert 159
Platters 56
Pop Code 126, 128
Popplestone Allen 129
Praetorian Guard 18
Presley, Elvis 33, 34, 35, 47, 53
Private Military Contractors (PMCs) 156
Private Security Industry Act (2001) 131
Public Entertainment Licence (PEL) 129
Purple Guide 128

Rainbow Theatre, Finsbury Park 69
Ray, Johnnie 34, 57
RCA 34
Reeves, Christopher 159
Regular Music 76
Reliance Security Services 88
Richard, Cliff 35, 47
Richard, Keith 36
Risk assessment 133
Ritchie, Guy 158
Ritchie, Jean 151
Riverfront Coliseum 101
Robins, Joyce 24
Robinson, Annette 58
Rock Steady 75-78, 99, 158
Roe, Tommy 57
Rolling Stones 36, 52, 53, 60, 136, 137
Roman games 13
Roskilde Festival 101
Roth, David Lee 103, 106, 110
Roxy 35
Royal Albert Hall 20
Royal Ballroom, Tottenham 48
Royal Victoria Theatre 26

Safety Advisory Group (SAG) 130
Safety at Sports Grounds Act 1975 122
Savage, Jon 29

Schleyerhalle Stadium, Stuttgart 148
Securicor 55
Security Industry Authority 121, 131
Shaughnessy, John 130
Shea Stadium, New York 59
Sheehan, Mick 16, 83
Show & Event Security 75, 88, 89
Showsec 9, 11, 68, 71, 75, 77-95, 100, 102,
        105, 107, 109, 144, 149, 150, 159,
        160
Showsec Training Centre 83, 135, 143,
        151, 163
SIA CP Licence 169
Sinatra, Frank 29, 34, 149
Six-Five Special 35
Slater, Gerry 56, 57, 62, 63, 66, 71, 77, 78,
        81, 82, 89, 94, 108
Smith, Julia 157
Smith, Mike 147
Soul, David 53, 151
Special Events Security Ltd 96
St. John Ambulance 105, 109, 127
Stardust Disco, Dublin 124
Starlite Artistes 51
Stephens, Basil 155
Stewart, Rod 159
Stopher, Superintendent Jed 171
Strutt, Pat 92, 93
Summerland 124
Sunday Pictorial 34
Super Stars 78
Super Teams 78
Surrey Gardens Music Hall 26
Swap Shop 78

Talit, Yahuda 111
Talit Productions 111
Taplin, Oliver 13
Tate, Sharon 145, 146
Taylor Report 87, 97, 123
Teddy Boy 33, 35, 49
Ted Heath Band 30
Temple of Dionysus 13
Thatched Barn Disco 48
Theatre Royal, Exeter 25

Theatre Royal Drury Lane 160
The Comets 33
The Embassy 69
The Shadows 35
The Who 61, 62, 135
Time Out 80
Tobler, John 34
Toft, Brian 125, 140, 167
Turner, Barry 167

United Kingdom Crowd Management
        Association (UKCMA) 100
University of Leicester 16
University of Victoria, British Columbia
        23

Valentine, Dickie 30
Valentine, Richard 31
Variety 25-28
Victoria Hall Theatre, Sunderland 25
Vince, Ron 79

Walker, Billy 50
Walker, Dave 31
Walsh, Peter 51
Webster, Charlie 40, 41
Wembley Stadium 18, 81, 88
Wham! 82, 161
Wheatley, Rt. Hon. Lord 122
Whelan, Bernadette 127
White, Sergeant Chris 171
White City Stadium 62, 126
Wicks, Jim 50
Wigg, David 160
Wilde, Marty 35
Wiles, David 20, 21
Willits, Alan 77
Wise, Kathy 86, 87
Wise, Nicola 86
Wise, Roy 83, 95
Wise, Terry 85, 87, 88, 100
World Chess Championship 144
Wright, Sergeant Tony 171

Zappa, Frank 148

ENTERTAINMENT TECHNOLOGY PRESS

FREE SUBSCRIPTION SERVICE

Keeping Up To Date with

From Ancient Rome to Rock 'n' Roll

Entertainment Technology titles are continually up-dated, and all major changes and additions are listed in date order in the relevant dedicated area of the publisher's website. Simply go to the front page of www.etnow.com and click on the BOOKS button. From there you can locate the title and be connected through to the latest information and services related to the publication.

The author of the title welcomes comments and suggestions about the book and can be contacted by email at:
mick.upton@btopenworld.com

Titles Published by Entertainment Technology Press

ABC of Theatre Jargon *Francis Reid* **£9.95** ISBN 1904031099
This glossary of theatrical terminology explains the common words and phrases that are
used in normal conversation between actors, directors, designers, technicians and managers.

Aluminium Structures in the Entertainment Industry *Peter Hind* **£24.95**
ISBN 1904031064
Aluminium Structures in the Entertainment Industry aims to educate the reader in all aspects
of the design and safe usage of temporary and permanent aluminium structures specific to
the entertainment industry – such as roof structures, PA towers, temporary staging, etc.

AutoCAD – A Handbook for Theatre Users *David Ripley* **£24.95** ISBN 1904031315
From 'Setting Up' to 'Drawing in Three Dimensions' via 'Drawings Within Drawings', this
compact and fully illustrated guide to AutoCAD covers everything from the basics to full colour
rendering and remote plotting.

Basics – A Beginner's Guide to Lighting Design *Peter Coleman* **£9.95** ISBN 1904031412
The fourth in the author's 'Basics' series, this title covers the subject area in four main
sections: The Concept, Practical Matters, Related Issues and The Design Into Practice. In an
area that is difficult to be difinitive, there are several things that cross all the boundaries of
all lighting design and it's these areas that the author seeks to help with.

Basics – A Beginner's Guide to Special Effects *Peter Coleman* **£9.95** ISBN 1904031331
This title introduces newcomers to the world of special effects. It describes all types
of special effects including pyrotechnic, smoke and lighting effects, projections, noise
machines, etc. It places emphasis on the safe storage, handling and use of pyrotechnics.

Basics – A Beginner's Guide to Stage Lighting *Peter Coleman* **£9.95** ISBN 190403120X
This title does what it says: it introduces newcomers to the world of stage lighting. It will
not teach the reader the art of lighting design, but will teach beginners much about the 'nuts
and bolts' of stage lighting.

Basics: A Beginner's Guide to Stage Management *Peter Coleman* **£7.95**
ISBN 9781904031475
The fifth in Peter Coleman's popular 'Basics' series, this title provides a practical insight
into, and the definition of, the role of stage management. Further chapters describe Cueing
or 'Calling' the Show (the Prompt Book), and the Hardware and Training for Stage
Management. This is a book about people and systems, without which most of the technical
equipment used by others in the performance workplace couldn't function.

Basics – A Beginner's Guide to Stage Sound *Peter Coleman* **£9.95** ISBN 1904031277
This title does what it says: it introduces newcomers to the world of stage sound. It will not
teach the reader the art of sound design, but will teach beginners much about the background
to sound reproduction in a theatrical environment.

Building Better Theaters *Michael Mell* **£16.95** 1904031404
A title within our Consultancy Series, this book describes the process of designing a theater,

from the initial decision to build through to opening night. Michael Mell's book provides a step-by-step guide to the design and construction of performing arts facilities. Chapters discuss: assembling your team, selecting an architect, different construction methods, the architectural design process, construction of the theater, theatrical systems and equipment, the stage, backstage, the auditorium, ADA requirements and the lobby. Each chapter clearly describes what to expect and how to avoid surprises. It is a must-read for architects, planners, performing arts groups, educators and anyone who may be considering building or renovating a theater.

Case Studies in Crowd Management
Chris Kemp, Iain Hill, Mick Upton, Mark Hamilton **£16.95** ISBN 9781904031482
This important work has been compiled from a series of research projects carried out by the staff of the Centre for Crowd Management and Security Studies at Buckinghamshire Chilterns University College, and seminar work carried out in Berlin and Groningen with partner Yourope. It includes case studies, reports and a crowd management safety plan for a major outdoor rock concert, safe management of rock concerts utilising a triple barrier safety system and pan-European Health & Safety Issues.

Close Protection – The Softer Skills *Geoffrey Padgham* **£11.95** ISBN 1904031390
This is the first educational book in a new 'Security Series' for Entertainment Technology Press, and it coincides with the launch of the new 'Protective Security Management' Foundation Degree at Buckinghamshire Chilterns University College (BCUC). The author is a former full-career Metropolitan Police Inspector from New Scotland Yard with 27 years' experience of close protection (CP). For 22 of those years he specialised in operations and senior management duties with the Royalty Protection Department at Buckingham Palace, followed by five years in the private security industry specialising in CP training design and delivery. His wealth of protection experience comes across throughout the text, which incorporates sound advice and exceptional practical guidance, subtly separating fact from fiction. This publication is an excellent form of reference material for experienced operatives, students and trainees.

A Comparative Study of Crowd Behaviour at Two Major Music Events
Chris Kemp, Iain Hill, Mick Upton **£7.95** ISBN 1904031250
A compilation of the findings of reports made at two major live music concerts, and in particular crowd behaviour, which is followed from ingress to egress.

Copenhagen Opera House *Richard Brett and John Offord* **£32.00** ISBN 1904031420
Completed in a little over three years, the Copenhagen Opera House opened with a royal gala performance on 15th January 2005. Built on a spacious brown-field site, the building is a landmark venue and this book provides the complete technical background story to an opera house set to become a benchmark for future design and planning. Sixteen chapters by relevant experts involved with the project cover everything from the planning of the auditorium and studio stage, the stage engineering, stage lighting and control and architectural lighting through to acoustic design and sound technology plus technical summaries.

Electrical Safety for Live Events *Marco van Beek* **£16.95** ISBN 1904031285
This title covers electrical safety regulations and good pracitise pertinent to the entertainment industries and includes some basic electrical theory as well as clarifying the "do's and don't's" of working with electricity.

The Exeter Theatre Fire *David Anderson* **£24.95** ISBN 1904031137
This title is a fascinating insight into the events that led up to the disaster at the Theatre Royal, Exeter, on the night of September 5th 1887. The book details what went wrong, and the lessons that were learned from the event.

Fading Light – A Year in Retirement *Francis Reid* **£14.95** ISBN 1904031358
Francis Reid, the lighting industry's favourite author, describes a full year in retirement. "Old age is much more fun than I expected," he says. Fading Light describes visits and experiences to the author's favourite theatres and opera houses, places of relaxation and re-visits to scholarly intitutions.

Focus on Lighting Technology *Richard Cadena* **£17.95** ISBN 1904031145
This concise work unravels the mechanics behind modern performance lighting and appeals to designers and technicians alike. Packed with clear, easy-to-read diagrams, the book provides excellent explanations behind the technology of performance lighting.

The Followspot Guide *Nick Mobsby* **£28.95** ISBN 9781904031499
The first in ETP's Equipment Series, Nick Mobsby's Followspot Guide tells you everything you need to know about followspots, from their history through to maintenance and usage. It's pages include a technical specification of 193 followspots from historical to the latest 2007 versions from major manufacturers.

Health and Safety Aspects in the Live Music Industry *Chris Kemp, Iain Hill* **£30.00** ISBN 1904031226
This title includes chapters on various safety aspects of live event production and is written by specialists in their particular areas of expertise.

Health and Safety Management in the Live Music and Events Industry *Chris Hannam* **£25.95** ISBN 1904031307
This title covers the health and safety regulations and their application regarding all aspects of staging live entertainment events, and is an invaluable manual for production managers and event organisers.

Hearing the Light – 50 Years Backstage *Francis Reid* **£24.95** ISBN 1904031188
This highly enjoyable memoir delves deeply into the theatricality of the industry. The author's almost fanatical interest in opera, his formative period as lighting designer at Glyndebourne and his experiences as a theatre administrator, writer and teacher make for a broad and unique background.

An Introduction to Rigging in the Entertainment Industry *Chris Higgs* **£24.95** ISBN 1904031129
This book is a practical guide to rigging techniques and practices and also thoroughly covers safety issues and discusses the implications of working within recommended guidelines and regulations.

Let There be Light – Entertainment Lighting Software Pioneers in Interview *Robert Bell* **£32.00** ISBN 1904031242
Robert Bell interviews a distinguished group of software engineers working on entertainment lighting ideas and products.

Lighting for Roméo and Juliette *John Offord* **£26.95** ISBN 1904031161
John Offord describes the making of the Vienna State Opera production from the lighting designer's viewpoint – from the point where director Jürgen Flimm made his decision not to use scenery or sets and simply employ the expertise of LD Patrick Woodroffe.

Lighting Systems for TV Studios *Nick Mobsby* **£45.00** ISBN 1904031005
Lighting Systems for TV Studios, now in its second edition, is the first book specifically written on the subject and has become the 'standard' resource work for studio planning and design covering the key elements of system design, luminaires, dimming, control, data networks and suspension systems as well as detailing the infrastructure items such as cyclorama, electrical and ventilation. Sensibly TV lighting principles are explained and some history on TV broadcasting, camera technology and the equipment is provided to help set the scene! The second edition includes applications for sine wave and distributed dimming, moving lights, Ethernet and new cool lamp technology.

Lighting Techniques for Theatre-in-the-Round *Jackie Staines* **£24.95**
ISBN 1904031013
Lighting Techniques for Theatre-in-the-Round is a unique reference source for those working on lighting design for theatre-in-the-round for the first time. It is the first title to be published specifically on the subject, it also provides some anecdotes and ideas for more challenging shows, and attempts to blow away some of the myths surrounding lighting in this format.

Lighting the Stage *Francis Reid* **£14.95** ISBN 1904031080
Lighting the Stage discusses the human relationships involved in lighting design – both between people, and between these people and technology. The book is written from a highly personal viewpoint and its 'thinking aloud' approach is one that Francis Reid has used in his writings over the past 30 years.

Model National Standard Conditions *ABTT/DSA/LGLA* **£20.00** ISBN 1904031110
These *Model National Standard Conditions* covers operational matters and complement *The Technical Standards for Places of Entertainment*, which describes the physical requirements for building and maintaining entertainment premises.

Mr Phipps' Theatre *Mark Jones, John Pick* **£17.95** ISBN: 1904031382
Mark Jones and John Pick describe "The Sensational Story of Eastbourne's Royal Hippodrome" – formerly Eastbourne Theatre Royal. An intriguing narrative, the book sets the story against a unique social history of the town. Peter Longman, former director of The Theatres Trust, provides the Foreword.

Pages From Stages *Anthony Field* **£17.95** ISBN 1904031269
Anthony Field explores the changing style of theatres including interior design, exterior design, ticket and seat prices, and levels of service, while questioning whether the theatre still exists as a place of entertainment for regular theatre-goers.

Performing Arts Technical Training Handbook 2007/2008 *ed: John Offord* **£19.95** ISBN 9781904031451
Published in association with the ABTT (Association of British Theatre Technicians), this important Handbook includes fully detailed and indexed entries describing courses on backstage crafts offered by over 100 universities and colleges across the UK. A completely

new research project, with accompanying website, the title also includes articles with advice for those considering a career 'behind the scenes', together with contact information and descriptions of the major organisations involved with industry training – plus details of companies offering training within their own premises. The Handbook will be kept in print, with a major revision annually.

Practical Dimming *Nick Mobsby* **£22.95** ISBN 19040313447
This important and easy to read title covers the history of electrical and electronic dimming, how dimmers work, current dimmer types from around the world, planning of a dimming system, looking at new sine wave dimming technology and distributed dimming. Integration of dimming into different performance venues as well as the necessary supporting electrical systems are fully detailed. Significant levels of information are provided on the many different forms and costs of potential solutions as well as how to plan specific solutions. Architectural dimming for the likes of hotels, museums and shopping centres are included. Practical Dimming is a companion book to Practical DMX and is designed for all involved in the use, operation and design of dimming systems.

Practical DMX *Nick Mobsby* **£16.95** ISBN 1904031368
In this highly topical and important title the author details the principles of DMX, how to plan a network, how to choose equipment and cables, with data on products from around the world, and how to install DMX networks for shows and on a permanently installed basis. The easy style of the book and the helpful fault finding tips, together with a review of different DMX testing devices provide an ideal companion for all lighting technicians and system designers. An introduction to Ethernet and Canbus networks are provided as well tips on analogue networks and protocol conversion. This title has been recently updated to include a new chapter on Remote Device Management that became an international standard in Summer 2006.

Practical Guide to Health and Safety in the Entertainment Industry
Marco van Beek **£14.95** ISBN 1904031048
This book is designed to provide a practical approach to Health and Safety within the Live Entertainment and Event industry. It gives industry-pertinent examples, and seeks to break down the myths surrounding Health and Safety.

Production Management *Joe Aveline* **£17.95** ISBN 1904031102
Joe Aveline's book is an in-depth guide to the role of the Production Manager, and includes real-life practical examples and 'Aveline's Fables' – anecdotes of his experiences with real messages behind them.

Rigging for Entertainment: Regulations and Practice *Chris Higgs* **£19.95**
ISBN 1904031218
Continuing where he left off with his highly successful *An Introduction to Rigging in the Entertainment Industry*, Chris Higgs' second title covers the regulations and use of equipment in greater detail.

Rock Solid Ethernet *Wayne Howell* **£24.95** ISBN 1904031293
Although aimed specifically at specifiers, installers and users of entertainment industry systems, this book will give the reader a thorough grounding in all aspects of computer networks, whatever industry they may work in. The inclusion of historical and technical 'sidebars' make for an enjoyable as well as informative read.

Sixty Years of Light Work *Fred Bentham* **£26.95** ISBN 1904031072
This title is an autobiography of one of the great names behind the development of modern stage lighting equipment and techniques.

Sound for the Stage *Patrick Finelli* **£24.95** ISBN 1904031153
Patrick Finelli's thorough manual covering all aspects of live and recorded sound for performance is a complete training course for anyone interested in working in the field of stage sound, and is a must for any student of sound.

Stage Lighting Design in Britain: The Emergence of the Lighting Designer, 1881-1950 *Nigel Morgan* **£17.95** ISBN 190403134X
This book sets out to ascertain the main course of events and the controlling factors that determined the emergence of the theatre lighting designer in Britain, starting with the introduction of incandescent electric light to the stage, and ending at the time of the first public lighting design credits around 1950. The book explores the practitioners, equipment, installations and techniques of lighting design.

Stage Lighting for Theatre Designers *Nigel Morgan* **£17.95** ISBN 1904031196
This is an updated second edition of Nigel Morgan's popular book for students of theatre design – outlining all the techniques of stage lighting design.

Technical Marketing Techniques *David Brooks, Andy Collier, Steve Norman* **£24.95** ISBN 190403103X
Technical Marketing is a novel concept, recently defined and elaborated by the authors of this book, with business-to-business companies competing in fast developing technical product sectors.

Technical Standards for Places of Entertainment *ABTT/DSA* **£30.00** ISBN 1904031056
Technical Standards for Places of Entertainment details the necessary physical standards required for entertainment venues.

Theatre Engineering and Stage Machinery *Toshiro Ogawa* **£30.00** ISBN 9781904031024
Theatre Engineering and Stage Machinery is a unique reference work covering every aspect of theatrical machinery and stage technology in global terms, and across the complete historical spectrum. Revised February 2007.

Theatre Lighting in the Age of Gas *Terence Rees* **£24.95** ISBN 190403117X
Entertainment Technology Press has republished this valuable historic work previously produced by the Society for Theatre Research in 1978. *Theatre Lighting in the Age of Gas* investigates the technological and artistic achievements of theatre lighting engineers from the 1700s to the late Victorian period.

Theatre Space: A Rediscovery Reported *Francis Reid* **£19.95** ISBN 1904031439
In the post-war world of the 1950s and 60s, the format of theatre space became a matter for a debate that aroused passions of an intensity unknown before or since. The proscenium arch was clearly identified as the enemy, accused of forming a barrier to disrupt the relations between the actor and audience. An uneasy fellow-traveller at the time, Francis Reid later recorded his impressions whilst enjoying performances or working in theatres old and new and this book is an important collection of his writings in various theatrical journals from

1969-2001 including his contribution to the Cambridge Guide to the Theatre in 1988. It reports some of the flavour of the period when theatre architecture was rediscovering its past in a search to establish its future.

Theatres of Achievement *John Higgins* **£29.95** ISBN: 1904031374
John Higgins affectionately describes the history of 40 distinguished UK theatres in a personal tribute, each uniquely illustrated by the author. Completing each profile is colour photography by Adrian Eggleston.

Theatric Tourist *Francis Reid* **£19.95** ISBN 9781904031468
Theatric Tourist is the delightful story of Francis Reid's visits across more than 50 years to theatres, theatre museums, performances and even movie theme parks. In his inimitable style, the author involves the reader within a personal experience of venues from the Legacy of Rome to theatres of the Renaissance and Eighteenth Century Baroque and the Gustavian Theatres of Stockholm. His performance experiences include Wagner in Beyreuth, the Pleasures of Tivoli and Wayang in Singapore. This is a 'must have' title for those who are as "incurably stagestruck" as the author.

Walt Disney Concert Hall – The Backstage Story *Patricia MacKay & Richard Pilbrow* **£28.95** ISBN 1904031234
Spanning the 16-year history of the design and construction of the Walt Disney Concert Hall, this book provides a fresh and detailed behind the scenes story of the design and technology from a variety of viewpoints. This is the first book to reveal the "process" of the design of a concert hall.

Yesterday's Lights – A Revolution Reported *Francis Reid* **£26.95** ISBN 1904031323
Set to help new generations to be aware of where the art and science of theatre lighting is coming from – and stimulate a nostalgia trip for those who lived through the period, Francis Reid's latest book has over 350 pages dedicated to the task, covering the 'revolution' from the fifties through to the present day. Although this is a highly personal account of the development of lighting design and technology and he admits that there are 'gaps', you'd be hard put to find anything of significance missing.

Go to www.etbooks.co.uk for full details of above titles and secure online ordering facilities.